BY
Elizabeth Baird
AND
The Food Writers of Canadian Living Magazine
and The Canadian Living Test Kitchen

A MADISON PRESS BOOK
PRODUCED FOR
BALLANTINE BOOKS AND CANADIAN LIVING™

Ballantine Books
A Division of
Random House of
Canada Limited
1265 Aerowood Drive
Mississauga, Ontario
Canada
L4W 1B9

Canadian Living
Telemedia
Communications Inc.
25 Sheppard Avenue West
Suite 100
North York, Ontario
Canada
M2N 6S7

Canadian Cataloguing in Publication Data

One-dish meals

(Canadian Living's best)
ISBN 0-345-39799-1

1. Entrées (Cookery).   I. Baird, Elizabeth.
II. Series.

TX740.5.E38 1994   641.8'2   C94-930271-6

EDITORIAL DIRECTOR: Hugh Brewster

PROJECT EDITOR: Wanda Nowakowska

EDITORIAL ASSISTANCE: Beverley Renahan

PRODUCTION DIRECTOR: Susan Barrable

PRODUCTION COORDINATOR: Donna Chong

BOOK DESIGN AND LAYOUT: Gordon Sibley Design Inc.

COLOR SEPARATION: Colour Technologies

PRINTING AND BINDING: Friesen Printers

CANADIAN LIVING ADVISORY BOARD: Elizabeth Baird, Bonnie Baker Cowan, Anna Hobbs,
Caren King, Greg MacNeil, Kirk Shearer

CANADIAN LIVING'S™ BEST ONE-DISH MEALS
was produced by Madison Press Books
under the direction of Albert E. Cummings

Madison Press Books
40 Madison Avenue
Toronto, Ontario, Canada
M5R 2S1

Printed in Canada

Contents

Introduction

Just add a leafy green salad and a loaf of crusty bread.

Now doesn't that conjure up the picture of a perfect meal, especially in the fall and winter? Something bubbling away in a Dutch oven or simmering in a soup pot. Maybe a pot pie or casserole dish baking to a crisp and golden brown on top while the middle layers mellow in the heat of the oven. All just waiting for the complementary tang of a vinaigrette, the crunch of greens and lots of fresh bread for sopping up the delicious juices that are part and parcel of stews, pot roasts, hearty soups and luscious casseroles.

And don't forget the tasty new takes on one-dish meals — stir-fries, convenient big-time sandwiches and satisfying whole-meal salads chock-full of lean meat, fish, chicken or vegetarian with beans, lentils and grains.

These are the kinds of substantial dishes you'll find in *Canadian Living's Best One-Dish Meals* — all with a healthy emphasis on eating increased amounts of vegetables and grains while cutting back on unnecessary fat. Rich with appealing and approachable flavors from around the world, these are meals you'll enjoy preparing yourself. We've streamlined the methods and simplified the cooking techniques so that even a cook new to the kitchen can produce a fine stew or time-saving stir-fry. Wherever possible, cooking times have also been reduced to turn what's normally been a long, slow cook into something faster and more manageable for today's busy households.

Many of the dishes are also make-ahead and freezable, with big-batch recipes as well as fuss-free dishes for one or two. And when it's time to bring the steaming pot, casserole or sandwich supper to the table, you'll agree that one-dish cooking is definitely in tune with the times.

Elizabeth Baird

*Stuffed Squash with Ham
and Rice (recipe, p. 10)*

Cosy Casseroles

No wonder casseroles are a cook's best friend. They're make-ahead, chock-full of old-fashioned slow-baked flavor, and equally delicious for weekday meals or weekend entertaining. They're also a great way to use up leftovers.

Country Cabbage Rolls ▶

Cabbage rolls rank high on everyone's list of wonderful no-pretense cooking. Our nineties-style version is richly flavored with beef, herbs and onions, then given a long tasty bake in sauerkraut and tomato juice. Cabbage rolls come with a bonus, too — they taste even better the second day! Serve with a dollop of sour cream and baked potatoes.

2	heads cabbage, cored (each 2 lb/1 kg)	2
1-1/4 cups	chicken stock	300 mL
1/2 cup	parboiled rice	125 mL
8	strips bacon, finely chopped	8
2 tbsp	butter	25 mL
3	onions, chopped	3
2	cloves garlic, minced	2
1/2 cup	finely chopped sweet red pepper	125 mL
1-1/2 tsp	dried marjoram	7 mL
1/2 tsp	dried thyme	2 mL
1-1/2 lb	lean ground beef	750 g
1/2 cup	chopped fresh parsley	125 mL
3/4 tsp	salt	4 mL
1/2 tsp	pepper	2 mL
1	egg, beaten	1
1	can (28 oz/796 mL) sauerkraut, rinsed and squeezed dry	1
3 tbsp	packed brown sugar	50 mL
1	can (48 oz/1.36 L) tomato juice	1

● In large pot of boiling salted water, blanch cabbage, one at a time, for 5 to 8 minutes or until leaves are softened. Remove and chill in cold water. Remove a few outer leaves and set aside.

● Working from core end, carefully remove 12 leaves from each cabbage, returning cabbage to boiling water for 2 to 3 minutes when leaves become difficult to remove. Drain on towels. Pare off coarse veins; set leaves aside.

● Meanwhile, in saucepan, bring stock to boil; stir in rice. Cover and cook over low heat for 15 to 20 minutes or until tender and stock is absorbed. Transfer to large bowl.

● Meanwhile, in skillet, cook bacon over medium heat for about 5 minutes or until crisp; drain off fat. Add butter to skillet; cook onions, garlic, red pepper, marjoram and thyme, stirring occasionally, for 5 minutes or until onions are softened. Add to rice along with beef, parsley, salt, pepper and egg; mix well.

● Spoon about 1/4 cup (50 mL) rice mixture onto each leaf just above stem. Fold end and sides over filling; roll up.

● Line 24-cup (6 L) roasting pan or Dutch oven with one-third of the sauerkraut; sprinkle with one-third of the sugar. Top with half of the rolls, seam side down. Cover with another third of the sauerkraut and another third of the sugar. Repeat with remaining rolls, sauerkraut and sugar.

● Pour tomato juice over top. Arrange a few reserved leaves over top to prevent scorching. Cover and bake in 350°F (180°C) oven for 1-1/2 hours. Uncover and bake for 30 minutes longer or until rolls are tender. Discard top leaves. Makes 8 servings.

Corn, Bean and Beef Casserole

All the fixings for beef burritos snuggle under a crusty kernel-studded corn bread. Serve with a zesty tomato, onion, cucumber and avocado salad. If you're lucky enough to have leftovers, tightly wrapped individual portions of this casserole freeze well and make great lunch or quick supper reheatables.

1 tbsp	olive oil	15 mL
1	onion, chopped	1
2	cloves garlic, minced	2
1/2 cup	each chopped celery and carrot	125 mL
1-1/2 lb	lean ground beef	750 g
3 tbsp	chili powder	50 mL
1-1/2 tsp	dried oregano	7 mL
1/4 tsp	each salt and pepper	1 mL
1	can (28 oz/796 mL) tomatoes, mashed	1
1/2 cup	chopped green olives	125 mL
1	can (19 oz/540 mL) red kidney beans, drained and rinsed	1
	TOPPING	
2 cups	corn kernels	500 mL
1 cup	all-purpose flour	250 mL
1 cup	milk	250 mL
1/2 cup	cornmeal	125 mL
1	egg	1
2 tbsp	butter, melted	25 mL
2-1/2 tsp	baking powder	12 mL
1/2 tsp	salt	2 mL
1-1/2 cups	shredded Monterey Jack or Cheddar cheese	500 mL
1/4 cup	chopped fresh coriander	50 mL

● In large saucepan, heat oil over medium heat; cook onion and garlic, stirring occasionally, for 3 minutes.

● Add celery, carrot, beef, chili powder, oregano, salt and pepper; cook, breaking up meat with back of spoon, for 7 to 10 minutes or until beef is no longer pink. Skim off fat.

● Stir in tomatoes and olives; bring to boil. Reduce heat to low; simmer for 5 minutes. Stir in kidney beans; pour into greased 13- x 9-inch (3 L) baking dish.

● TOPPING: In bowl, whisk together corn, flour, milk, cornmeal, egg, butter, baking powder and salt; pour evenly over filling. Sprinkle with cheese.

● Bake in 400°F (200°C) oven for 35 to 40 minutes or until puffy and golden around edges. Let stand for 10 minutes; sprinkle with coriander. Makes 8 servings.

TIP: When fresh coriander (also known as cilantro or Chinese parsley) can't be found, you can substitute fresh parsley, although the flavor is not the same. To get closer to the allure of fresh coriander, add some of its dried counterpart, available in jars where quality spices and herbs are sold under the herb's Spanish name, "cilantro."

CASSEROLE DISHES

● Avoid **metal dishes** as they are thin, can discolor and impart a metallic taste to the food.

● **Heatproof glass baking dishes** in standard sizes are extremely useful for oven and microwave cooking. Do not heat on top of the stove or under the broiler.

● **Pottery and porcelain casseroles** are attractive, especially for carrying to potlucks. While ovenproof, the casseroles generally cannot be used under a broiler or on top of the stove, although they are excellent for reheating in the microwave. Store and handle carefully to avoid breaking.

● **Enameled cast-iron casseroles** and gratin dishes last for years and go happily from stovetop to oven to freezer and table.

Shepherd's Hash Brown Pie ▲

2 tsp	vegetable oil	10 mL
1	onion, chopped	1
1	clove garlic, minced	1
1 lb	lean ground beef	500 g
1 tbsp	chili powder	15 mL
1 tsp	dried oregano	5 mL
1/2 tsp	each salt and pepper	2 mL
1	can (19 oz/540 mL) stewed tomatoes	1
1-1/2 cups	frozen mixed chopped vegetables	375 mL
	TOPPING	
3 cups	frozen hash brown potatoes	750 mL
1 cup	shredded Cheddar cheese	250 mL
Pinch	each salt and pepper	Pinch
1	egg, beaten	1

● In large skillet, heat oil over medium heat; cook onion and garlic, stirring occasionally, for 3 minutes. Add beef, chili powder, oregano, salt and pepper; cook, breaking up meat with back of spoon, for about 5 minutes or until beef is no longer pink.

● Add tomatoes, breaking up further with spoon; bring to boil. Reduce heat and simmer for about 15 minutes or until thickened. Stir in vegetables. Spoon into greased 10-inch (25 cm) pie plate.

● TOPPING: In bowl, toss together potatoes, Cheddar, salt and pepper; stir in egg until combined. Spoon evenly over meat mixture. Bake in 400°F (200°C) oven for 30 minutes. Broil for about 3 minutes or until topping is golden. Makes 4 servings.

Ready-made frozen hash browns make a conveniently different topping instead of the usual mashed spuds. Frozen chopped vegetables are another time-saver.

Souffléed Ham, Swiss Cheese and Squash

Puffy and light, this tasty casserole is a great way to use up leftover ham. Other smoked meats such as turkey or chicken taste good, too.

2 tbsp	butter	25 mL
1	onion, chopped	1
1/4 cup	all-purpose flour	50 mL
1 cup	milk	250 mL
1/4 tsp	pepper	1 mL
Pinch	each cayenne pepper and nutmeg	Pinch
1-1/2 cups	shredded Emmenthal cheese	375 mL
2	eggs, separated	2
2 cups	mashed cooked pepper squash	500 mL
1/2 tsp	salt	2 mL
2 cups	diced Black Forest ham	500 mL
1/2 cup	coarse fresh bread crumbs	125 mL

● In saucepan, melt butter over medium heat; cook onion, stirring occasionally, for 3 minutes or until softened. Sprinkle with flour; cook, stirring, for 1 minute. Stir in milk, pepper, cayenne and nutmeg; cook, stirring, for about 4 minutes or until thickened. Stir in 1 cup (250 mL) of the cheese until melted.

● In bowl, beat egg yolks with fork; stir in a little of the cheese sauce. Stir mixture back into pan; cook, stirring, for 2 minutes. Pour into bowl; add squash and salt, mixing well.

● In separate bowl, beat egg whites until stiff peaks form; stir about 1 cup (250 mL) into squash mixture. Fold in remaining egg whites.

● Sprinkle ham in 8-cup (2 L) baking dish; spread squash mixture evenly over top. Combine bread crumbs with remaining cheese; sprinkle over casserole. Bake in 375°F (190°C) oven for 40 to 45 minutes or until puffed and golden. Makes 6 servings.

TIP: You'll need about a 2-lb (1 kg) squash to yield 2 cups (500 mL) cooked and mashed. (See Stuffed Squash with Ham and Rice, below, for instructions on cooking squash.)

Stuffed Squash with Ham and Rice

Although cooking for one or two is a challenge, there are some simple tricks that make meal planning easier — like making more than enough rice for one meal and using the leftovers to make this cheese-and-ham stuffed squash.

1	acorn squash (about 2 lb/1 kg)	1
	Salt and pepper	
1 cup	cooked rice	250 mL
2	slices Black Forest ham, slivered (4 oz/125 g)	2
1	can (10 oz/284 mL) stewed tomatoes, drained	1
Pinch	each hot pepper flakes and dried oregano	Pinch
1/2 cup	shredded mozzarella cheese	125 mL

● Cut squash in half lengthwise; seed and place, cut side down, in microwaveable baking dish. Add 2 tbsp (25 mL) water; cover and microwave at High for 8 minutes or until almost tender. Season with salt and pepper to taste.

● Meanwhile, in large bowl, toss together rice, ham, tomatoes, hot pepper flakes and oregano; mound in squash cavities. Microwave, uncovered, at High for 3 minutes or until heated through. Sprinkle with mozzarella; microwave for 45 seconds or until cheese melts. Makes 2 servings.

TIP: To bake instead of microwave, place halved squash in baking dish; cover with foil and bake in 350°F (180°C) oven for 40 to 45 minutes or until almost tender. Mound rice mixture in cavities; bake for 15 minutes. Sprinkle with mozzarella; bake for 5 minutes.

Creole Sausage and Peppers

2-1/2 cups	brown rice (or 2 cups/500 mL parboiled white)	625 mL
1-1/2 lb	spicy Italian sausage	750 g
1 tbsp	vegetable oil	15 mL
1/4 cup	water	50 mL
4	sweet peppers, coarsely chopped	4
3	onions, coarsely chopped	3
3	stalks celery, thickly sliced	3
3	cloves garlic, minced	3
1	bay leaf	1
1/2 tsp	each dried thyme and oregano	2 mL
1/4 tsp	pepper	1 mL
Pinch	(approx) cayenne pepper	Pinch
Pinch	salt	Pinch
2	cans (each 19 oz/540 mL) tomatoes	2
1/3 cup	chopped fresh parsley	75 mL
1	can (19 oz/540 mL) chick-peas, drained	1
2/3 cup	freshly grated Parmesan cheese	150 mL

● In large pot of boiling salted water, cook rice until tender but firm, about 45 minutes for brown, 20 minutes for white. Drain and rinse; drain again and place in large bowl.

● Meanwhile, prick sausage. In large Dutch oven, heat oil over medium heat; cook sausage, in batches if necessary, for 8 to 10 minutes or until browned. Add water; reduce heat, cover and simmer for 10 minutes or until firm. Cut diagonally into 1/4-inch (5 mm) thick slices; set aside.

● Drain off all but 2 tbsp (25 mL) liquid in pan. Add sweet peppers, onions, celery and garlic; cook, stirring occasionally, for 5 minutes or until softened. Stir in bay leaf, thyme, oregano, pepper, cayenne and salt; cook for 1 minute.

● Add tomatoes, breaking up with back of spoon. Add sausages; bring to boil. Reduce heat and simmer for 15 minutes or until vegetables are tender. Discard bay leaf. Stir in parsley. Season with more cayenne, if desired.

● Remove 1 cup (250 mL) tomato sauce from sausage mixture; add to reserved rice along with chick-peas and toss to combine. Spread in two 8-inch (2 L) square baking dishes; top with sausage mixture. Sprinkle with Parmesan. *(Recipe can be prepared to this point and cooled in refrigerator; cover and store for up to 1 day or freeze for up to 2 months. Thaw completely. Bake for 30 minutes longer than specified.)*

● Bake, loosely covered, in 350°F (180°C) oven for 30 minutes; uncover and bake for 15 minutes longer or until golden and heated through. Makes 8 servings.

Perfect for at-home entertaining or on-location potlucks, this robust casserole serves eight generously — or freezes in smaller portions for two or more meals.

Speedy Choucroute Garni ▶

Pressure cooking makes short work of this Alsatian classic, mingling tangy sauerkraut, smoky sausages and apples into a satisfying one-pot meal in minutes — instead of the usual hours.

1 tbsp	vegetable oil	15 mL
4	pork loin chops (3/4 inch/2 cm thick)	4
8 oz	kielbasa sausage	250 g
1 cup	white wine, beer or chicken stock	250 mL
1	bay leaf	1
5	juniper berries	5
4 cups	sauerkraut, drained	1 L
3	large apples, peeled and thickly sliced	3
1	large onion, chopped	1
2	cloves garlic, minced	2
1 tbsp	caraway seeds	15 mL
1/2 tsp	pepper	2 mL
1/4 tsp	ground cloves	1 mL
4 oz	smoked ham, cubed	125 g
4	large potatoes, peeled and quartered	4
1/4 tsp	salt	1 mL
	Parsley sprigs	
	Red apple, sliced	

● In pressure cooker, heat oil over medium-high heat; brown pork chops, in batches, for 3 minutes per side. Remove and set aside.

● Cut sausage into 1/2-inch (1 cm) thick slices; add to cooker and cook, turning often, for 2 minutes or until crisp. Remove and set aside.

● Add wine, bay leaf and juniper berries, stirring to scrape up brown bits; remove from heat. Arrange half of the sauerkraut in cooker. Top with half each of the apples, onion and garlic; top with chops. Sprinkle with half each of the caraway seeds, pepper and cloves.

● Layer with remaining sauerkraut, apple, onion and garlic. Arrange sausage and ham over top. Sprinkle with remaining caraway seeds, pepper and cloves. Top with potatoes; sprinkle with salt. Lock lid.

● Over high or medium heat (depending upon manufacturer's directions), bring to high pressure. Decrease heat according to manufacturer's directions, maintaining high pressure for 10 minutes.

● Place pressure cooker in sink; run cold water over lid for about 2 minutes to quick-release all pressure. Release lid lock slowly to allow remaining steam to escape. With slotted spoon, arrange choucroute on platter, discarding bay leaf. Garnish with parsley and apple slices. Serve with pan juices. Makes 6 to 8 servings.

TIP: To bake choucroute instead of pressure-cooking, use large Dutch oven and follow recipe but set browned pork chops aside along with potatoes. Cover and bake remaining ingredients in 350°F (180°C) oven for 1-1/2 hours. Nestle chops in mixture; top with potatoes. Cover and bake, basting twice, for 45 minutes or until potatoes are tender.

PRESSURE COOKERS

An important part of the modern kitchen years ago, pressure cookers are taking "center stove" again in the '90s. The latest versions, with their sleek look and foolproof locks, are ideal for stewing — giving long-simmered flavor in a very short time. Check the manufacturer's instructions for adapting other one-dish recipes for pressure cooking.

Tex-Mex Potato Casserole

Stock up on ground beef when it's on special to make family-pleasing dishes like this layered potato and chili-flavored casserole. Repack bulk family packs into 1-lb (500 g) lots in freezer bags. Don't forget to date, label and use within two to three months.

1 lb	lean ground beef	500 g
1	onion, chopped	1
2	cloves garlic, minced	2
1 tbsp	chili powder	15 mL
1/4 tsp	each ground cumin, hot pepper flakes, dried oregano and salt	1 mL
1	can (19 oz/540 mL) stewed tomatoes	1
1	sweet green pepper, diced	1
1/3 cup	chopped pitted black olives	75 mL
4	potatoes (unpeeled), thinly sliced	4
1 tbsp	all-purpose flour	15 mL
1 tbsp	vegetable oil	15 mL
1 cup	shredded Cheddar cheese	250 mL
2	green onions, sliced	2

● In large skillet, cook beef, onion and garlic over medium heat, breaking up meat with back of spoon, for about 5 minutes or until beef is no longer pink. Skim off fat.

● Stir in chili powder, cumin, hot pepper flakes, oregano and salt; cook, stirring, for 1 minute. Stir in tomatoes; cook, stirring occasionally, for 20 minutes or until thickened. Stir in green pepper and olives.

● Meanwhile, in 11- x 7-inch (2 L) baking dish, toss together potatoes, flour and oil; spread evenly in dish. Spoon meat mixture over top; cover and bake in 350°F (180°C) oven for about 45 minutes or until potatoes are tender.

● Sprinkle with Cheddar; bake for 5 minutes or until melted. Sprinkle green onions around edge. Makes 4 servings.

Pizza Popover

A winner in Canadian Living's first Family Supper Contest, Maureen Jewell described this puffy, golden upside-down pizza as a favorite with her children — and a great substitute for take-out pizza.

1 lb	lean ground beef	500 g
1/2 cup	chopped onion	125 mL
1/2 cup	chopped sweet red or green pepper	125 mL
1	small clove garlic, minced	1
1/2 tsp	dried oregano	2 mL
Dash	hot pepper sauce	Dash
1	can (10 oz/284 mL) sliced mushrooms	1
1	can (7-1/2 oz/213 mL) tomato sauce	1
1 cup	shredded mozzarella cheese	250 mL
1/4 cup	freshly grated Parmesan cheese (optional)	50 mL
	POPOVER	
1/2 cup	milk	125 mL
1 tsp	vegetable oil	5 mL
1	egg	1
1/2 cup	all-purpose flour	125 mL
1/4 tsp	salt	1 mL

● In large skillet, cook beef, onion, red pepper, garlic, oregano and hot pepper sauce over medium heat, breaking up meat with back of spoon, for about 5 minutes or until beef is no longer pink. Skim off fat.

● Add mushrooms and tomato sauce; simmer for 10 minutes or until slightly thickened. Pour into 9-inch (2.5 L) square cake pan; sprinkle with mozzarella.

● POPOVER: In small bowl, beat together milk, oil and egg for 1 minute. Add flour and salt; beat for 2 minutes. Pour evenly over mozzarella, covering completely. Sprinkle with Parmesan (if using).

● Bake in 400°F (200°C) oven for 25 to 30 minutes or until puffed and golden brown. Makes 4 servings.

Shepherd's Pie with Garlic Mashed Potatoes

2 tbsp	vegetable oil	25 mL
1	onion, chopped	1
2	cloves garlic, minced	2
1	stalk celery, chopped	1
1	sweet red pepper, chopped	1
1	carrot, chopped	1
3 cups	sliced mushrooms (8 oz/250 g)	750 mL
1-1/2 lb	lean ground beef	750 g
1/2 cup	chili sauce	125 mL
1/2 cup	ketchup	125 mL
	Salt and pepper	
	TOPPING	
4	large potatoes (about 2 lb/1 kg), peeled and cubed	4
2 tbsp	butter	25 mL
4	cloves garlic, minced	4
1/2 cup	milk	125 mL
1 tsp	salt	5 mL
1/2 tsp	pepper	2 mL
1 tsp	paprika	5 mL

● In large skillet, heat oil over medium heat; cook onion and garlic for 2 to 3 minutes or until softened but not browned. Add celery, red pepper, carrot and mushrooms; cook, stirring occasionally, for 7 minutes or until all liquid has evaporated.

● Add beef; cook over medium-high heat, breaking up meat with back of spoon, for 7 to 10 minutes or until lightly browned. Skim off fat.

● Add chili sauce and ketchup; bring to boil. Reduce heat to low; simmer for 10 minutes. Season with salt and pepper to taste. Transfer to 11- x 7-inch (2 L) baking dish.

● TOPPING: Meanwhile, in saucepan of boiling salted water, cook potatoes for about 20 minutes or until tender; drain well.

● Meanwhile, in small skillet, melt butter over low heat; cook garlic for 5 minutes or until fragrant and tender but not browned. Add to potatoes along with milk, salt and pepper; mash until smooth.

● Spread or pipe potatoes over meat mixture; sprinkle with paprika. Bake in 350°F (180°C) oven for 30 to 40 minutes or until filling is bubbly and topping is golden. Makes 6 servings.

Cooked garlic adds a mellow sweetness to the mashed potatoes topping this new-fashioned shepherd's pie. Keep these mashed potatoes in mind as a tasty side with stews and roasts, too.

WHICH GROUND BEEF IS BEST?

● Nowadays, lean ground beef, with no more than 17% fat by weight, is a popular choice for casseroles, chilies and stews. Medium, with no more than 23% fat by weight, is second choice — especially in summer when it's often on sale. Regular ground beef, with no more than 30% fat by weight, as well as medium ground are best suited to burgers or dishes where fat drips off during cooking.

● When cooking any kind of ground beef, try to remove as much fat as possible. The easiest way to do this is to tip the skillet, push sautéed meat and vegetables to one side and skim off fat with a large shallow spoon. Or, if you have a long-spouted gravy separator, pour contents of pan through sieve into separator. Return solids to skillet; allow liquid to settle, then pour it back, discarding the fat that remains in the separator.

Microwave Chinese Chicken and Rice ▼

The microwave incorporates all the flavors of a pleasing stir-fry plus rice — and conveniently steam-cooks them all in one dish.

1 lb	boneless skinless chicken	500 g
2 cups	water	500 mL
1 cup	parboiled rice	250 mL
1/2 tsp	(approx) salt	2 mL
1-1/2 cups	broccoli florets	375 mL
1 cup	sliced mushrooms	250 mL
	Pepper	
	MARINADE	
2 tbsp	vegetable oil	25 mL
4 tsp	cornstarch	20 mL
1 tbsp	minced gingerroot	15 mL
2 tsp	soy sauce	10 mL
1/2 tsp	salt	2 mL
1/2 tsp	granulated sugar	2 mL
1	clove garlic, minced	1
Dash	hot pepper sauce	Dash

● MARINADE: In bowl, combine oil, cornstarch, ginger, soy sauce, salt, sugar, garlic and hot pepper sauce. Cut chicken into 1-inch (2.5 cm) cubes; add to bowl. Cover and marinate at room temperature for 30 minutes.

● In 12-cup (3 L) microwaveable casserole, combine water, rice and salt; cover and microwave at High for 4 to 7 minutes or until water boils. Microwave at Medium (50%) for 7 minutes.

● Add chicken mixture, broccoli and mushrooms; cover and microwave at Medium (50%), rotating dish once, for 7 to 9 minutes or until liquid is absorbed and chicken is no longer pink inside. Let stand for 5 minutes. Season with salt and pepper to taste. Makes 4 servings.

Crusty Chicken Cassoulet

3 cups	great Northern beans	750 mL
8 oz	lean bacon, chopped	250 g
4 lb	chicken thighs	2 kg
4	carrots, sliced	4
4	cloves garlic, slivered	4
2	large onions, chopped	2
2	stalks celery, chopped	2
1	can (28 oz/796 mL) tomatoes	1
3 cups	(approx) chicken stock	750 mL
1	bay leaf	1
1 tsp	dried rosemary	5 mL
1/2 tsp	each dried thyme, salt and pepper	2 mL
	TOPPING	
4 cups	fresh bread crumbs	1 L
1/2 cup	chopped fresh parsley	125 mL
1/4 cup	butter, softened	50 mL

● Sort and rinse beans, discarding any blemished ones. In large saucepan, cover beans with 3 times their volume of water; bring to boil and cook for 2 minutes. Remove from heat; cover and let stand for 1 hour. Drain.

● Cover beans with 3 times their new volume of fresh water; bring to boil. Reduce heat, cover and simmer for 1 hour or until tender; drain.

● Meanwhile, in large Dutch oven, cook bacon over medium-high heat until crisp; remove and reserve. Drain off all but 1 tbsp (15 mL) fat from pan. Add chicken, in batches if necessary, and brown all over; remove and reserve. Drain off fat.

● Reduce heat to medium-low; cook carrots, garlic, onions and celery, stirring occasionally, for 8 minutes or until softened. Add tomatoes, breaking up with back of spoon. Add chicken stock, bay leaf, rosemary, thyme, salt and pepper, stirring to scrape up brown bits.

● Add beans, reserved bacon and chicken; bring to boil. Reduce heat, partially cover and simmer for 45 minutes or until slightly thickened. Discard bay leaf. If serving immediately, mash some of the beans to thicken sauce. Transfer to 24-cup (6 L) casserole. (*Cassoulet can be prepared to this point, cooled in refrigerator and stored in airtight container for up to 1 day or frozen for up to 2 months. Thaw before continuing; add 1 hour to baking time.*)

● TOPPING: Mix bread crumbs, parsley and butter; sprinkle over cassoulet.

● Bake in 350°F (180°C) oven for 1 hour or until crusty and golden on top, bubbly and heated through. Makes 8 servings.

TIP: To make fresh bread crumbs, cut crusts off Italian or other crusty bread; break, a few slices at a time, into chunks and place in food processor. Pulse until crumbly. If you like the crusts and they are not too hard, leave them on.

Beans team up with bacon, chicken, vegetables and tomatoes in a crusty crumb-topped winner of a casserole. Add a creamy cabbage and carrot slaw and thickly sliced sourdough bread for cosy cold-weather entertaining.

BROWNING MEAT

● When browning chicken or meat, always do it in batches, in a heavy-bottomed shallow Dutch oven or skillet over high or medium-high heat, making sure there's plenty of room in the pan so meat does not steam and stew.

● Transfer meat as it browns onto a plate, adding oil to pan if necessary. When returning meat to the pan for its final cooking, be sure to include all the juices that have accumulated on the plate.

Asparagus Lasagna ▼

Here's your chance to trade in your lasagna meat sauce for a fresh asparagus filling. (See TIP on trimming asparagus, p. 46.)

4 lb	asparagus	2 kg
1/3 cup	butter	75 mL
1/2 cup	all-purpose flour	125 mL
5 cups	milk	1.25 L
8 oz	creamy goat cheese (chèvre)	250 g
1 tsp	grated lemon rind	5 mL
1 tbsp	lemon juice	15 mL
1-1/2 tsp	salt	7 mL
1/2 tsp	pepper	2 mL
1/4 tsp	nutmeg	1 mL
15	lasagna noodles (about 12 oz/375 g)	15
2 cups	shredded mozzarella cheese	500 mL
1/3 cup	freshly grated Parmesan cheese	75 mL

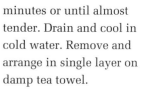

● Trim asparagus; cut stalks into 1-inch (2.5 cm) pieces. In large pot of boiling water, cook asparagus for 3 minutes. Drain and refresh under cold water; drain again. Remove 1-1/2 cups (375 mL) asparagus tips; set aside.

● In saucepan, melt butter over medium heat; whisk in flour and cook, whisking, for 1 minute. Gradually whisk in milk; bring to boil.

● Reduce heat to medium-low; cook, stirring, for 10 minutes or until thickened. Remove from heat. Stir in goat cheese, lemon rind and juice, salt, pepper and nutmeg until cheese has melted.

● Meanwhile, in large pot of boiling salted water, cook noodles for 6 to 8 minutes or until almost tender. Drain and cool in cold water. Remove and arrange in single layer on damp tea towel.

● Arrange 3 noodles in single layer in greased 13-x 9-inch (3 L) baking dish. Spread with 1 cup (250 mL) of the sauce, then one-quarter of the asparagus, then one-quarter of the mozzarella. Repeat layers 3 more times. Top with final layer of noodles and sauce. Sprinkle Parmesan over top.

● Bake in 375°F (190°C) oven for 35 to 40 minutes or until light golden and bubbly. Sprinkle reserved asparagus tips over top. Bake for 5 minutes or until asparagus is heated through. Let stand for 10 minutes before serving. Makes 8 servings.

Marsetti ▼

Half	pkg (375 g) egg noodles	Half
1 lb	lean ground beef	500 g
1	onion, chopped	1
1	sweet green pepper, chopped	1
1	can (10 oz/284 mL) mushroom pieces, drained	1
2	cans (each 14 oz/398 mL) tomato sauce or spaghetti sauce	2
1/2 tsp	each salt and pepper	2 mL
6 oz	Cheddar cheese, cubed	175 g

● In large pot of boiling salted water, cook noodles for 8 to 10 minutes or until tender but firm; drain well.

● Meanwhile, in large skillet, cook beef over medium-high heat, breaking up with back of spoon, for about 4 minutes or until no longer pink; skim off fat.

● Add onion and green pepper; cook, stirring often, for about 3 minutes or until softened. Add mushrooms, tomato sauce, salt and pepper. Reserve 1/2 cup (125 mL) of the Cheddar for topping; stir remaining Cheddar into skillet.

● Spoon meat mixture into 12-cup (3 L) casserole dish; add noodles and gently stir to combine. Sprinkle with reserved Cheddar. Cover and bake in 350°F (180°C) oven for 30 minutes or until bubbly. If desired, broil for 2 minutes to brown cheese. Makes 6 servings.

This is the kind of old favorite that every casserole collection should contain. It's fast, easy and delicious. What more could you ask of a weeknight supper? Serve with a salad and slices of homemade garlic bread (see box, p. 62).

Cheese and Mushroom Perogy Casserole

3	lasagna noodles	3
6	large potatoes, peeled	6
1/2 cup	milk	125 mL
1	egg	1
1 cup	cottage cheese	250 mL
2	green onions, chopped	2
	Salt and pepper	
1 tbsp	butter	15 mL
1	onion, chopped	1
4 cups	sliced mushrooms about (8 oz/250 g)	1 L
3/4 cup	shredded old orange Cheddar cheese	175 mL
2 tbsp	dry bread crumbs	25 mL

● In large pot of boiling salted water, cook noodles for 6 to 8 minutes or until almost tender. With tongs, remove noodles and cool in cold water. Remove and arrange in single layer on damp tea towel.

● Add potatoes to pot; cover and cook for about 20 minutes or until fork-tender. Drain and return to low heat for 30 seconds to dry. Mash thoroughly; mash in milk and egg. Stir in cottage cheese and green onions; season with salt and pepper to taste.

● Meanwhile, in skillet, melt butter over medium-low heat; cook onion and mushrooms, stirring occasionally, for about 20 minutes or until softened and most of the liquid has evaporated. Season with salt and pepper to taste.

● Spread half of the potato mixture in greased 8-inch (2 L) square baking dish. Cover with half of the noodles, cutting to fit. Spread with mushroom mixture. Cover with remaining noodles, then potatoes. Sprinkle with Cheddar and bread crumbs. Bake in 400°F (200°C) oven for about 20 minutes or until lightly puffed and golden brown. Makes 4 servings.

Layers of mashed potatoes, mushrooms and lasagna noodles deliver all the comfort of stuffed perogies — with a lot less work! A bright green salad with a mustardy dressing is a must alongside. Individual servings reheat beautifully in the microwave.

Party-Size Baked Vegetable Spaghetti

Buffets nowadays call for at least one vegetarian dish. This one is sure to win raves from everyone.

2 tbsp	olive oil	25 mL
2	large onions, chopped	2
3	cloves garlic, minced	3
4	zucchini, diced	4
1	each sweet green and yellow pepper, diced	1
1	eggplant, peeled and diced	1
2	cans (each 19 oz/540 mL) tomatoes	2
1	can (5-1/2 oz/156 mL) tomato paste	1
2 tsp	dried basil	10 mL
1 tsp	each dried oregano, granulated sugar and salt	5 mL
1/2 tsp	pepper	2 mL
1/4 tsp	dried thyme	1 mL
1 lb	spaghetti	500 g
1/4 cup	freshly grated Parmesan cheese	50 mL
	CHEESE SAUCE	
1/4 cup	butter	50 mL
1/4 cup	all-purpose flour	50 mL
2 cups	milk	500 mL
1 cup	shredded mozzarella cheese	250 mL
1/2 tsp	salt	2 mL
1/4 tsp	pepper	1 mL

● In Dutch oven, heat half of the oil over medium-high heat; cook onions, garlic, zucchini, sweet peppers and eggplant, stirring often, for 5 to 10 minutes or until starting to soften.

● Add tomatoes, tomato paste, basil, oregano, sugar, salt, pepper and thyme; bring to boil. Reduce heat and simmer for 25 to 30 minutes or until slightly thickened.

● CHEESE SAUCE: Meanwhile, in saucepan, melt butter over medium heat; whisk in flour and cook, whisking, for 2 minutes, without browning. Gradually whisk in milk and bring to boil; reduce heat to medium-low and cook, whisking, for about 10 minutes or until thickened. Stir in mozzarella, salt and pepper; cook, stirring, until cheese has melted.

● Meanwhile, in large pot of boiling salted water, cook spaghetti for 5 minutes or until still very firm. Drain and toss with remaining olive oil and vegetable mixture.

● Transfer spaghetti mixture to 13-x 9-inch (3 L) baking dish; spoon cheese sauce over top. Sprinkle with Parmesan. *(Casserole can be prepared to this point, cooled in refrigerator, covered and stored for up to 1 day. Or, wrap tightly and freeze for up to 2 weeks. Thaw in refrigerator for 48 hours. Add 10 minutes to baking time.)*

● Bake on baking sheet in 350°F (180°C) oven for about 1 hour or until golden and bubbly. Makes 8 servings.

HOW MUCH DO I BUY?

● **A pound (500 g) of white mushrooms**, trimmed but still with stems, slices into 6 cups (1.5 L). For each cup (250 mL), buy about 3 oz (100 g). However, since the quantity of mushrooms is often not crucial in a recipe, it is often easier to round the amount up and be a little generous.

● **A pound (500 g) of firm cheese** such as mozzarella, Cheddar, Swiss or Monterey Jack shreds into 4 cups (1 L). So, for every cup (250 mL), buy 4 oz (125 g).

Fiesta Mac and Cheese ▼

2 cups	macaroni	500 mL
2 tbsp	butter	25 mL
3 tbsp	all-purpose flour	45 mL
1 tsp	dry mustard	5 mL
1/2 tsp	salt	2 mL
1/4 tsp	pepper	1 mL
2 cups	milk	500 mL
2 cups	shredded Cheddar cheese	500 mL
1	can (114 mL) jalapeño peppers, rinsed and chopped	1
1 tsp	Worcestershire sauce	5 mL
1 tbsp	vegetable oil	15 mL
1/4 cup	chopped green onions	50 mL
1 tsp	chili powder	5 mL
1 tsp	dried oregano	5 mL
1	can (7-1/2 oz/213 mL) tomato sauce	1
	Chopped green onion tops	

● In large pot of boiling salted water, cook macaroni for 8 to 10 minutes or until tender but firm. Drain well; return to pot.

● Meanwhile, in separate saucepan, melt butter over medium heat; whisk in flour, mustard, salt and pepper. Cook, whisking, for 2 minutes, without browning. Gradually whisk in milk and bring to boil; reduce heat to medium-low and cook, whisking, for about 5 minutes or until thickened.

● Remove from heat; stir in 1-1/2 cups (375 mL) of the Cheddar, jalapeño peppers and Worcestershire sauce until Cheddar has melted. Stir into macaroni. Pour into greased 8-cup (2 L) casserole; bake in 375°F (190°C) oven for 25 to 30 minutes or until golden brown and bubbly.

● Meanwhile, in small saucepan, heat oil over medium heat; cook green onions, chili powder and oregano for 1 minute. Stir in tomato sauce and bring to boil; partially cover, reduce heat and simmer for 10 minutes. Spoon over baked macaroni. Sprinkle with remaining Cheddar and green onion tops. Makes 4 to 6 servings.

A *plateful of macaroni and cheese pushes all the right buttons — comfort, cheer, warmth and simple pleasure. This one has a south-of-the-border twist fans are sure to enjoy. So will kids who like Mexican-style food. Serve with a green bean salad.*

Vegetarian Moussaka Doubles ▶

Here's a handy Greek custard-topped casserole that makes enough for eight. Divide it into two dishes — one casserole to eat right away, the other to freeze for later. Individual portions, tightly wrapped and frozen, make excellent emergency suppers or lunches. Complement the eggplant, feta cheese and chunky tomato sauce of the casserole with garlic bread and a cucumber salad.

4	eggplant (3-1/2-lb/1.75 kg total)	4
1 tbsp	salt	15 mL
1/4 cup	olive oil	50 mL
2 cups	shredded feta cheese	500 mL
	CUSTARD	
1/4 cup	butter	50 mL
1/4 cup	all-purpose flour	50 mL
1-1/2 cups	milk	375 mL
1 tsp	salt	5 mL
1/4 tsp	each nutmeg and pepper	1 mL
4	eggs	4
2 cups	ricotta or cottage cheese	500 mL
	TOMATO SAUCE	
2 tbsp	olive oil	25 mL
3	onions, chopped	3
2	zucchini, diced	2
1	sweet red pepper, diced	1
4	cloves garlic, minced	4
2 tsp	dried oregano	10 mL
3/4 tsp	cinnamon	4 mL
1/4 tsp	pepper	1 mL
1	can (19 oz/540 mL) tomatoes, drained and chopped	1
1	can (5-1/2 oz/156 mL) tomato paste	1

● Cut eggplant into 1/2-inch (1 cm) thick slices. Layer in colander, sprinkling each layer with salt; let stand for 30 minutes. Rinse and drain well; pat dry.

● In batches, brush eggplant with oil and broil on baking sheet, turning once, for 8 to 12 minutes or until lightly browned. Set aside.

● CUSTARD: Meanwhile, in saucepan, melt butter over medium heat; whisk in flour and cook, whisking, for 2 minutes, without browning. Gradually whisk in milk until smooth; cook, whisking often, for 2 to 4 minutes or until boiling and thickened. Season with salt, nutmeg and pepper. Transfer to large bowl; let cool slightly. Blend in eggs and ricotta.

● TOMATO SAUCE: In large skillet, heat oil over medium heat; cook onions, zucchini, red pepper and garlic, stirring occasionally, for about 5 minutes or until softened. Stir in oregano, cinnamon and pepper; cook, stirring, for 1 minute. Add tomatoes and tomato paste; bring to boil. Reduce heat and simmer for 10 minutes or until zucchini is tender.

● Spread one-quarter of the tomato sauce in each of two 8-inch (2 L) square baking dishes; top each with one-quarter of the eggplant. Sprinkle each with 1/2 cup (125 mL) of the feta. Top with remaining tomato sauce, then remaining eggplant. Spread custard over top; sprinkle with remaining feta. *(Moussaka can be prepared to this point, cooled in refrigerator, covered and stored for up to 1 day or frozen for up to 2 months. Thaw completely.)*

● Bake in 350°F (180°C) oven for 1 hour or until top is browned and set. Let stand for 15 minutes; cut into squares. Makes 8 servings.

Crunchy Crouton Quiche ▼

Croutons make a crunchy, low-fat pie crust for an economical and satisfying egg pie. A quiche pan makes the best-looking pie, but you can also bake it in a 10-inch (25 cm) pie plate — just increase the bread to 7 cups (1.75 L).

2 tsp	butter	10 mL
1	onion, chopped	1
2	cloves garlic, minced	2
1/2 tsp	dried thyme	2 mL
	Salt and pepper	
6 cups	cubed French or Italian bread (1/2-inch/1 cm cubes)	1.5 L
1/2 cup	chicken stock	125 mL
5	eggs	5
2 cups	broccoli florets	500 mL
2 cups	milk or light (10%) cream	500 mL
1 cup	shredded old Cheddar cheese	250 mL
1	carrot, sliced	1
Half	sweet red pepper, diced	Half

● In skillet, melt butter over medium heat; cook onion, garlic, thyme and pinch each salt and pepper, stirring occasionally, for 3 minutes or until softened. Transfer to large bowl.

● Add bread cubes and toss to combine. Pour in chicken stock and 1 of the eggs; toss to coat well. Gently pat mixture evenly onto bottom and side of greased 10-inch (25 cm) quiche dish to form shell. Bake in 425°F (220°C) oven for 10 minutes or until light golden.

● Meanwhile, in pot of boiling water, cook broccoli for 2 minutes. Drain and refresh under cold water; drain well and pat dry.

● In bowl, whisk together remaining eggs, milk and pinch each salt and pepper. Stir in broccoli, 3/4 cup (175 mL) of the Cheddar, the carrot and red pepper; pour into baked shell. Sprinkle with remaining Cheddar. Bake in 375°F (190°C) oven for about 40 minutes or until knife inserted in center comes out clean. Makes 6 servings.

Two-Cheese and Corn Baked Risotto

1 tbsp	butter	15 mL
1	onion, chopped	1
1 cup	each chopped sweet red and green pepper	250 mL
1 cup	Arborio or other short grain Italian rice	250 mL
2-1/2 cups	hot water	625 mL
2 cups	corn kernels	500 mL
1 cup	milk	250 mL
1	egg	1
2 tsp	all-purpose flour	10 mL
1-1/4 tsp	salt	6 mL
3/4 tsp	pepper	4 mL
2 cups	shredded white old Cheddar cheese	500 mL
1/3 cup	chopped fresh basil	75 mL
1	tomato, sliced	1
1 tbsp	freshly grated Parmesan cheese	15 mL

● In large saucepan, melt butter over medium heat; cook onion and red and green peppers, stirring occasionally, for 5 minutes. Add rice; cook, stirring, for 1 minute.

● Add water and corn; bring to boil. Reduce heat to low; cover and cook for about 15 minutes or until liquid is absorbed.

● Whisk together milk, egg, flour, salt and pepper; stir into rice mixture along with Cheddar and basil. Pour into greased 8-inch (2 L) square baking dish.

● Arrange tomato over top; sprinkle with Parmesan. Bake on baking sheet in 350°F (180°C) oven for 25 to 35 minutes or until liquid is absorbed. Let stand for 5 minutes. Makes 4 servings.

This summer-fresh, no-stir risotto keeps all the creaminess but takes the effort out of this classic Italian dish.

Tofu Ratatouille

1	eggplant	1
	Salt	
2 tbsp	olive oil	25 mL
1	onion, chopped	1
2	cloves garlic, minced	2
2	zucchini, cubed	2
1	can (28 oz/796 mL) tomatoes	1
1 tsp	salt	5 mL
1/2 tsp	pepper	2 mL
2 tbsp	chopped fresh basil (or 2 tsp/10 mL dried)	25 mL
1 tbsp	chopped fresh oregano, thyme or marjoram (or 1 tsp/5 mL dried)	15 mL
2 cups	well-drained regular tofu	500 mL
1 cup	shredded old Cheddar cheese	250 mL

● Cut eggplant into 1/2-inch (1 cm) cubes; place in colander. Sprinkle evenly with salt; let stand for 30 minutes. Rinse and drain well; pat dry.

● In saucepan, heat oil over medium heat; cook onion and garlic, stirring occasionally, for 3 minutes or until softened. Add zucchini; cook for 2 minutes.

● Add eggplant and tomatoes, breaking up tomatoes with back of spoon. Stir in salt and pepper. Simmer over low heat for 30 minutes or until thickened. Stir in basil and oregano. *(Ratatouille can be prepared to this point, cooled in refrigerator, covered and stored for up to 1 day.)*

● In blender or food processor, purée tofu with Cheddar; spread half in greased 8-cup (2 L) baking dish. Cover with half of the ratatouille. Repeat layers. Bake in 350°F (180°C) oven for about 30 minutes or until bubbly. Makes 4 servings.

Tofu is an excellent way to slip protein into a main-course vegetarian dish. It's also low in fat and calories and high in calcium (if you choose tofu firmed with calcium sulphate or calcium chloride). Add a green salad and a loaf of crusty bread, preferably whole grain, and no one will miss the meat.

Big-Batch Impossible Broccoli Pie

The Canadian Living Test Kitchen created this recipe for community kitchens, where a group can get together and make a number of suppers to take home to their families. If the quantity doesn't suit your household, the recipe divides easily in half, using 4 eggs and 1 yolk. Half serves six, or fewer with leftovers for lunches.

1/2 cup	dry bread crumbs	125 mL
1-1/4 lb	ham, cut into 1/2-inch (1 cm) cubes	625 g
4 cups	shredded Cheddar or Monterey Jack cheese	1 L
2	large onions, chopped	2
3 cups	corn kernels	750 mL
3/4 tsp	pepper	4 mL
1/2 tsp	dry mustard	2 mL
1/4 tsp	each chili powder and salt	1 mL
3 cups	broccoli florets	750 mL
1/4 cup	shortening	50 mL
1-1/4 cups	all-purpose flour	300 mL
1 tbsp	baking powder	15 mL
9	eggs	9
4 cups	milk	1 L

● Sprinkle bread crumbs evenly over bottom and sides of two greased 8-inch (2 L) square baking dishes.

● In large bowl, combine ham, Cheddar, onions, corn, pepper, mustard, chili powder and salt; sprinkle over bread crumbs. Arrange broccoli over top.

● In blender or food processor and using on/off motion, cut shortening into flour and baking powder until in fine crumbs. Add eggs and 1 cup (250 mL) of the milk; blend until smooth. Stir in remaining milk; pour over ham mixture.

● Bake in 350°F (180°C) oven for 55 to 60 minutes or until set and knife inserted in center comes out clean. Let stand for 5 minutes before cutting. Makes 12 servings.

TIP: Instead of throwing away broccoli stalks, peel off the coarse fibrous skin and either cut into sticks for nibbling and dipping, or shred coarsely like cabbage and combine with shredded carrot for a slaw.

Red Pepper Cheese Quiche

R*emember how good quiche used to taste? It's time to revive those quiche tastebuds with this great weeknight supper. Serve with a green salad and fruit for dessert.*

1	sweet red pepper	1
1	baked 9-inch (23 cm) pie shell (recipe, p. 33)	1
1 tbsp	Dijon mustard	15 mL
4 oz	herbed cream cheese, cut into bits	125 g
2	eggs	2
3/4 cup	milk	175 mL
1/4 tsp	each salt and pepper	1 mL
Pinch	nutmeg	Pinch
1 tbsp	chopped fresh basil (or 1 tsp/5 mL dried)	15 mL

● Broil red pepper, turning several times, for about 20 minutes or until blistered and charred. Let cool; peel, seed and cut into thin strips. Set aside.

● Brush pie shell with mustard; arrange cheese over top. Beat together eggs, milk, salt, pepper and nutmeg; pour over cheese. Sprinkle with basil; top with red pepper.

● Bake in 400°F (200°C) oven, shielding pastry with foil if necessary to prevent overbrowning, for 30 to 40 minutes or until puffy, golden and knife inserted in center comes out clean. Makes 6 servings.

SWEET-PEPPER PIZZAZZ

Sweet red, yellow and orange peppers contribute to any cook's repertoire. They punch up the color and zip up the taste of casseroles, stews and salads. However, when peppers are not in season, they are expensive, even the increasingly available ones grown in Canadian green-houses. You can replace red peppers with green, always cheaper but not quite as sweet. Roasted red peppers in jars are handy (no peeling and seeding) and a slightly cheaper choice.

Spicy Rice and Beans ▼

1 tbsp	vegetable oil	15 mL
2	cloves garlic, minced	2
1	onion, chopped	1
1 cup	long grain brown rice	250 mL
1 tsp	ground cumin	5 mL
2 cups	vegetable stock	500 mL
1 cup	mild chunky salsa	250 mL
1	can (19 oz/540 mL) pinto, black or kidney beans, drained and rinsed	1
1-1/2 cups	corn kernels	375 mL
1/2 tsp	salt	2 mL
1/4 tsp	pepper	1 mL
1	can (19 oz/540 mL) Mexican Spice stewed tomatoes	1

● In Dutch oven, heat oil over medium-high heat; cook garlic and onion, stirring occasiona for 3 to 5 minutes or until softened. Stir in rice and cumin; cook, stirring, for 1 minute.

● Add stock, salsa, beans, corn, salt and pepper. Cover and bake in 350°F (180°C) oven for 45 minutes or until rice is tender (a little liquid will remain).

● Coarsely chop tomatoes; pour over rice. Bake for 10 to 15 minutes or until tomatoes are heated through. *(Casserole can be cooled in refrigerator and stored in airtight container for up to 5 days; reheat to serve.)* Makes 4 servings.

As with most bean recipes, you can choose the kind of beans you prefer. Serve a bowl of plain yogurt topped with chopped fresh coriander alongside this easy-to-fix vegetarian meal.

ONE-POT SIDE DISHES

● When cooking pasta or rice, add vegetables such as sliced carrots, cubed squash, broccoli or broccoflower florets, cabbage wedges, asparagus, sugar snap peas, beans, chard or spinach to the pot a few minutes before the pasta or rice is finished cooking and cook until both are ready.

● Drain and toss pasta or rice plus vegetable with a drizzle of olive oil or butter, a squirt of fresh lemon juice and some chopped fresh herbs.

● Although stronger-flavored vegetables can affect the taste of the pasta or rice, they are usually not in the water long enough to change the taste very much or cancel the convenience.

Cheesy Tuna Doubles

Tuna casserole gets a nifty new update with fresh spinach, curly pasta and the nippiest Cheddar available. This recipe makes enough for two casseroles. To make only one casserole, follow instructions below, dividing all amounts in half except for the butter in the sauce (use 3 tbsp/50 mL) and the tuna (use 1 can).

2	pkg (each 10 oz/284 g) fresh spinach, trimmed	2
1/3 cup	butter	75 mL
3	onions, chopped	3
1/2 cup	all-purpose flour	125 mL
6 cups	milk	1.5 L
2 tsp	each dried basil and salt	10 mL
1 tsp	pepper	5 mL
Pinch	hot pepper flakes	Pinch
4 cups	fusilli or penne	1 L
3	cans (each 7-1/2 oz/213 g) tuna, drained and broken into chunks	3
2 cups	shredded old Cheddar cheese	500 mL
2 tbsp	lemon juice	25 mL
	TOPPING	
3 cups	fresh bread crumbs	750 mL
1 cup	shredded old Cheddar cheese	250 mL
1 tbsp	butter, melted	15 mL
1 tbsp	Dijon mustard	15 mL

● Rinse spinach; shake off excess water. In stockpot, cover spinach and cook, with just the water clinging to leaves, over medium-high heat for about 5 minutes or until wilted. Drain well and squeeze dry; chop coarsely and set aside.

● In large saucepan, melt butter over medium heat; cook onions, stirring occasionally, for 3 minutes or until softened. Whisk in flour; cook, whisking, for 3 minutes, without browning.

Gradually whisk in milk until smooth; cook, whisking often, for about 15 minutes or until boiling and thickened. Reduce heat to low. Season with basil, salt, pepper and hot pepper flakes.

● Meanwhile, in large pot of boiling salted water, cook fusilli for 8 to 10 minutes or until tender but firm. Drain and refresh under cold water; drain again and return to pot.

● Add sauce, spinach, tuna, Cheddar and lemon juice; toss together. Divide between two greased 8-inch (2 L) square baking dishes, spreading evenly.

● TOPPING: Toss together bread crumbs, Cheddar, butter and mustard; sprinkle over casseroles. *(Casseroles can be prepared to this point, cooled in refrigerator, covered and stored for up to 1 day or frozen for up to 2 months. Thaw completely. Bake for 25 to 30 minutes longer than specified, uncovering only during last 10 minutes.)*

● Loosely cover and bake in 350°F (180°C) oven for 20 minutes; uncover and bake for 25 minutes longer or until heated through and golden. Makes 8 servings.

TIP: A package of frozen spinach is a convenient replacement for a bag of fresh spinach. Simply thaw and drain well, pressing out moisture.

Eggs Creole ▼

2 tsp	vegetable oil	10 mL
2 tbsp	chopped onion	25 mL
3 cups	sliced mushrooms (8 oz/250 g)	750 mL
1	stalk celery, chopped	1
1	large carrot, grated	1
1	can (28 oz/796 mL) tomatoes, chopped	1
1/2 tsp	each dried oregano and basil	2 mL
1/4 tsp	dried thyme	1 mL
Pinch	cayenne pepper	Pinch
	Salt	
3/4 cup	diced ham	175 mL
6	hard-cooked eggs, peeled and halved	6

● In large skillet, heat oil over medium heat; cook onion, stirring occasionally, for 2 minutes or until softened. Add mushrooms; cook, stirring, for 2 minutes.

● Stir in celery, carrot, tomatoes, oregano, basil, thyme, cayenne, and salt to taste; bring to boil. Reduce heat and simmer, stirring occasionally, for 30 to 35 minutes or until thickened. Stir in ham. Gently stir in eggs; heat through. Makes 6 servings.

A quick spicy tomato sauce turns hard-cooked eggs into a main course. Serve over parsleyed rice with a romaine lettuce salad.

Fast-Lane Chicken Pot Pie ▶

Even with something as "Mom" as chicken pot pie, it's still possible to cut a few corners. Leftover chicken saves time, as do frozen pie shells and vegetables. When time allows, make your own pastry (recipe, p. 33) and prepare your own selection of vegetables such as carrots, beans and potatoes.

2 tbsp	butter	25 mL
4	green onions, chopped	4
2 tbsp	all-purpose flour	25 mL
1 cup	chicken stock	250 mL
1/2 cup	milk	125 mL
3/4 tsp	salt	4 mL
1/2 tsp	dry mustard	2 mL
1/4 tsp	each pepper and dried thyme	1 mL
2 cups	frozen mixed chopped vegetables	500 mL
1-1/2 cups	chopped cooked chicken (see p. 76)	375 mL
1 cup	quartered canned potatoes	250 mL
2	frozen 9-inch (23 cm) deep-dish pie shells	2
1	egg, lightly beaten	1

● In large saucepan, melt butter over medium heat; cook onions, stirring occasionally, for 1 minute or until softened. Sprinkle with flour; cook, stirring, for 1 minute, without browning. Gradually whisk in stock and milk; bring to boil.

● Reduce heat and cook, stirring, for 5 minutes or until thickened. Stir in salt, mustard, pepper and thyme. Add frozen vegetables, chicken and potatoes. Pour filling into 1 of the pie shells.

● Moisten edge with some of the egg; invert remaining pie shell over top and remove foil plate. Flute edges to seal. Brush top with egg; cut steam vents in top. Bake in 400°F (200°C) oven for about 30 minutes or until filling is bubbly and crust is golden. Makes 4 servings.

Vegetable Cobbler

Here's a neat idea for a warming vegetarian entrée — a winter-crisper selection of veggies and mushrooms, napped in a thyme sauce and baked under a whole wheat drop-biscuit crust. Meat eaters can add diced ham, corned beef or leftover turkey or chicken.

1 tbsp	olive oil	15 mL
1	onion, chopped	1
1 cup	sliced mushrooms	250 mL
2	cloves garlic, minced	2
2 tbsp	all-purpose flour	25 mL
2 cups	vegetable stock	500 mL
1/2 tsp	dried thyme	2 mL
1/4 tsp	each salt and pepper	1 mL
2	potatoes, peeled and diced	2
3	carrots, diced	3
2	stalks celery, diced	2
1 cup	diced peeled rutabaga	250 mL
2 tbsp	chopped fresh parsley	25 mL
	BISCUIT CRUST	
1/3 cup	whole wheat flour	75 mL
1/3 cup	all-purpose flour	75 mL
1/3 cup	shredded Cheddar cheese	75 mL
1 tsp	baking powder	5 mL
1/4 tsp	baking soda	1 mL
1/4 tsp	salt	1 mL
1 tbsp	butter, melted	15 mL
1/2 cup	plain yogurt	125 mL

● In large saucepan, heat oil over medium heat; cook onion, mushrooms and garlic, stirring occasionally, for 3 minutes or until softened.

● Sprinkle with flour; cook, stirring, for 1 minute. Gradually stir in stock, thyme, salt and pepper; cook, stirring, for 5 minutes or until boiling and thickened.

● Add potatoes, carrots, celery and rutabaga; cover and simmer, stirring often, for 15 minutes or until tender-crisp. Stir in parsley. Spoon into 8-cup (2 L) casserole dish.

● BISCUIT CRUST: Meanwhile, in bowl, combine whole wheat and all-purpose flours, Cheddar, baking powder, baking soda and salt. Stir butter into yogurt; stir into flour mixture just until combined. Drop by large spoonfuls over vegetables.

● Bake in 375°F (190°C) oven for 25 to 30 minutes or until biscuit crust is golden. Let stand for 2 minutes. Makes 4 servings.

Chicken Pie with Phyllo Crust ▼

Phyllo pastry, found in the frozen food section near pie shells, updates a fine pot pie with a crisp, light topping. Once thawed, phyllo will keep in airtight wrapping for weeks in the refrigerator and can be used for tart shells, mini strudels and appetizers.

1/3 cup	butter	75 mL
1-1/2 cups	quartered mushrooms (about 4 oz/125 g)	375 mL
1	onion, chopped	1
1	clove garlic, minced	1
1/4 cup	all-purpose flour	50 mL
3 cups	chicken stock	750 mL
	Salt and pepper	
1/4 cup	chopped fresh parsley	50 mL
1 tsp	dried marjoram	5 mL
6 cups	chopped cooked chicken (see p. 76)	1.5 L
4 cups	cubed cooked carrots or parsnips (about 8)	1 L
1 cup	fresh or frozen peas	250 mL
5	sheets phyllo pastry	5

● In large saucepan, melt 2 tbsp (25 mL) of the butter over medium heat; cook mushrooms, onion and garlic, stirring occasionally, for 3 minutes or until softened. Stir in flour; cook, stirring, for 2 minutes.

● Gradually stir in stock and bring to boil; cook, stirring, for about 5 minutes or until thickened. Season with salt and pepper to taste; stir in parsley and marjoram. Remove from heat. Stir in chicken, carrots and peas. Pour into 13- x 9-inch (3.5 L) baking dish. Let cool completely.

● Melt remaining butter. Keeping remaining phyllo covered with damp tea towel to prevent drying out, place 1 sheet over chicken mixture, folding under excess to fit inside dish; lightly brush with butter. Repeat with remaining phyllo and butter. *(Pie can be prepared to this point, covered and refrigerated for up to 12 hours; bring to room temperature before continuing.)*

● Bake in 375°F (190°C) oven for 25 to 30 minutes or until pastry is golden and filling bubbly. Makes 4 servings.

TIP: One way to arrive at 3 cups (750 mL) chicken stock and 6 cups (1.5 L) chopped cooked chicken is to use canned broth and leftover chicken. Or, simmer 3 lb (1.5 kg) boneless chicken in 4 cups (1 L) water along with some flavorings such as a chopped onion, carrot and celery stalk plus a bay leaf and sprinkle of thyme for about 25 minutes or until chicken is no longer pink inside.

PERFECT PASTRY EVERY TIME

6 cups	cake-and-pastry flour (or 5-1/4 cups/1.3 L all-purpose flour)	1.5 L
1-1/2 tsp	salt	7 mL
2-1/3 cups	lard or shortening (1 lb/454 g)	575 mL
1	egg	1
1 tbsp	white vinegar	15 mL
	Ice water	

● In large bowl, combine flour with salt. Using pastry blender or 2 knives, cut in lard until mixture resembles fine crumbs with a few larger pieces.

● In measuring cup and using fork, beat together egg and vinegar until blended. Add enough ice water to make 1 cup (250 mL).

● Stirring briskly with fork, gradually add just enough egg mixture, 1 tbsp (15 mL) at a time, to flour mixture to make dough hold together. Divide into 6 portions and press each into ball. Wrap in plastic wrap and refrigerate for 30 minutes. *(Dough can be refrigerated for up to 1 week, or frozen for up to 3 months.)*

● Let cold pastry stand for 15 minutes at room temperature before rolling out. Makes enough for three 9-inch (23 cm) double-crust pies.

Mini Beef Pot Pies

1-1/2 lb	lean stewing beef	750 g
2 tbsp	vegetable oil	25 mL
1 cup	chopped onions	250 mL
2 cups	coarsely chopped mushrooms	500 mL
1/2 cup	chopped sweet green pepper	125 mL
2 tbsp	all-purpose flour	25 mL
2 cups	beef stock	500 mL
3	carrots, cut into chunks	3
1 tbsp	Worcestershire sauce	15 mL
1/2 tsp	dried thyme	2 mL
Pinch	cinnamon	Pinch
1	stalk celery	1
1	bay leaf	1
1 cup	frozen peas	250 mL
	Salt and pepper	
	Pastry for three 9-inch (23 cm) pie shells	
1	egg yolk	1

● Cut beef into 1-inch (2.5 cm) cubes, trimming off any fat. In Dutch oven, heat half of the oil over medium-high heat; brown beef for 6 to 8 minutes. Remove and set aside.

● Add onions and 1 tbsp (15 mL) water to pan; cook, stirring often, for 3 minutes or until golden. Add remaining oil, mushrooms and green pepper; cook, stirring often, for 4 minutes.

● Sprinkle with flour; cook, stirring, over medium heat for 1 minute. Gradually whisk in stock; cook, stirring, for 4 minutes or until thickened.

● Return beef to pan. Add carrots, Worcestershire sauce, thyme, cinnamon, celery and bay leaf; cover and bring to boil. Reduce heat to medium-low; simmer for 1 hour or until beef is tender. Discard celery and bay leaf. Add peas, and salt and pepper to taste. Let cool.

● On lightly floured surface, roll out pastry. Cut out 5 bottoms and 5 tops to fit 4-1/2- x 1-1/4-inch (11 x 3 cm) foil tart tins. Line tins with pastry bottoms; fill with beef mixture. Moisten edges of pastry with water; cover with pastry tops and press edges together with tines of fork to seal. Combine egg yolk with 1 tbsp (15 mL) water; brush over top. *(Pies can be prepared to this point, wrapped well and frozen for up to 1 month; bake, frozen, in 450°F /230°C oven for same amount of time.)*

● Cut steam vents in top; bake on baking sheet in 375°F (190°C) oven for 40 to 45 minutes or until crust is golden and filling is bubbly. Makes 5 servings.

These single-serving pies are perfect for small households or to sell at bazaars.

Wok and Skillet Suppers

These suppers are for action cooks! A tumble of fresh ingredients in a hot pan, a pinch of spices or herbs, a few quick tosses or stirs — and a delicious dinner is on its way to the table in no time at all.

Easy Chicken Stir-Fry ▶

A wok-full of crunchy vegetables and succulent chicken with enough glossy sauce to flavor a steaming bowl of rice — no wonder everyone loves a stir-fry. Keep the basics of this stir-fry in mind, then vary the ingredients to suit your taste or the occasion.

1	bunch broccoli	1
1	sweet red pepper	1
2	large green onions	2
3	boneless skinless chicken breasts	3
1/2 cup	chicken stock	125 mL
2 tbsp	soy sauce	25 mL
1 tbsp	cornstarch	15 mL
1 tbsp	oyster sauce	15 mL
1 tbsp	dry sherry	15 mL
1 tsp	sesame oil	5 mL
1/4 tsp	chili paste or dash hot pepper sauce (optional)	1 mL
3 tbsp	vegetable oil	50 mL
2	cloves garlic, minced	2
1 tbsp	minced gingerroot	15 mL
1/4 cup	halved cashew nuts (optional)	50 mL

● Cut broccoli into florets; peel and cut stalks on diagonal into 1/4-inch (5 mm) thick slices. Cut red pepper into 1-inch (2.5 cm) squares. Cut green onions in half lengthwise; cut on diagonal into 2-inch (5 cm) pieces. Cut chicken into thin strips. Set aside separately.

● Whisk together 1/4 cup (50 mL) of the chicken stock, soy sauce, cornstarch, oyster sauce, sherry, sesame oil, and chili paste (if using); set aside.

● Heat wok or deep skillet over high heat. Add half of the oil; heat for 30 seconds, swirling to coat pan. Stir-fry half of the chicken for 3 to 4 minutes or until no longer pink inside; remove and set aside. Repeat with remaining chicken, adding some of the oil if necessary. Add to reserved chicken.

● Add remaining oil to wok; stir-fry garlic and ginger for 10 seconds or until fragrant. Add broccoli and red pepper; stir-fry for 1 minute. Add onions; stir-fry for 30 seconds. Pour in remaining stock; cover and steam, stirring once, for 2 minutes or until broccoli is tender-crisp.

● Stir chicken back into wok; push to side of pan. Pour soy mixture into center of wok; cook, stirring, for 1 to 2 minutes or until thickened. Stir chicken mixture into sauce until coated. Sprinkle with cashew nuts (if using). Makes 4 servings.

VARIATION
● ORANGE BEEF STIR-FRY: Substitute 12 oz (375 g) thinly sliced sirloin for chicken; stir-fry for 2 to 3 minutes or until lightly browned but still pink inside. Substitute beef stock for chicken stock. Omit oyster sauce; add 1/4 cup (50 mL) orange juice and 1 tbsp (15 mL) grated orange rind. Substitute 1 tbsp (15 mL) sesame seeds for nuts.

Chicken Shepherd's Pie ▼

*G*round chicken or turkey,
now available in many
supermarkets, brings a
delicious new taste to an old
favorite. Cover the skillet's
handle with foil to make it
ovenproof, if necessary.

1 tsp	vegetable oil	5 mL
1	onion, chopped	1
1 lb	ground chicken	500 g
1 tbsp	all-purpose flour	15 mL
1/2 cup	chicken stock	125 mL
2 cups	frozen mixed vegetables, thawed and drained	500 mL
1/4 cup	chopped fresh parsley (or 4 tsp/20 mL dried)	50 mL
1 tbsp	ketchup	15 mL
1 tsp	Worcestershire sauce	5 mL
1/4 tsp	dried sage	1 mL
	Salt and pepper	
6	potatoes, peeled	6
1	egg	1
1/3 cup	light cottage cheese	75 mL

● In deep 10-inch (25 cm) nonstick ovenproof skillet, heat oil over medium heat; cook onion, stirring occasionally, for 3 minutes or until softened. Add chicken; cook, breaking up with back of spoon, for 5 to 7 minutes or until no longer pink. Sprinkle with flour; cook, stirring, for 1 minute. Gradually stir in chicken stock; cook, stirring, until thickened.

● Stir in vegetables, parsley, ketchup, Worcestershire sauce and sage; bring to boil. Reduce heat and simmer for 5 minutes. Season with salt and pepper to taste.

● Meanwhile, in saucepan of boiling water, cover and cook potatoes over medium-high heat for 15 to 20 minutes or until tender; drain and return to pot. Using potato masher, mash until smooth.

● Beat in egg and cottage cheese; season with salt and pepper to taste. Spoon over chicken mixture. Broil for 7 to 8 minutes or until golden. Makes 4 servings.

CAST-IRON SKILLETS

Cast-iron skillets still rank high for skillet suppers and require very little fat when cooking — as long as you keep them seasoned. The secret is never to use detergent when cleaning a cast-iron skillet. Swish in hot water, using a brush or nylon scouring pad to lift off stubborn bits, and soak, if necessary. Rinse well, wipe dry with sponge or dish cloth and let air-dry before storing in dry spot.

Stir-Fried Turkey and Fiddleheads

12 oz	boneless turkey or chicken breast	375 g
2 tbsp	(approx) vegetable oil	25 mL
1	onion, chopped	1
2	cloves garlic, minced	2
1 tbsp	minced gingerroot	15 mL
8 oz	fresh fiddleheads (about 25), cleaned	250 g
3 tbsp	oyster sauce	50 mL

● Cut turkey into thin strips; set aside.

● Heat large skillet over high heat; add 1 tbsp (15 mL) of the oil, swirling to coat pan. Stir-fry onion, garlic and ginger for 1 minute.

● Add turkey; stir-fry for 2 to 3 minutes or until no longer pink, adding more oil if necessary. Add fiddleheads; stir-fry for 2 minutes.

● Pour in 1/4 cup (50 mL) water and oyster sauce; reduce heat to medium-low. Cover and simmer, stirring occasionally, for 5 minutes or until fiddleheads are tender. Makes 4 servings.

TIP: When fiddleheads are out of season, substitute 1 package (10 oz/284 g) thawed frozen fiddleheads, if desired.

CLEANING FIDDLEHEADS

Cleaning fiddleheads is like shelling peas. The first step is to enlist help, especially when the quantities are large. Luckily, this particular stir-fry doesn't call for many fiddleheads and cleaning the ferns doesn't take long.
● To clean these edible Ostrich ferns (which grow over much of eastern Canada and are available in many farmers' markets and supermarkets in the spring), pick off the papery brown covering, one fiddlehead at a time. Trim off end of stem. It's a pleasant chore sitting outside, letting the spring breezes carry off the light brown coverings.

For a change of taste, replace the more exotic fiddleheads in this super-quick stir-fry with two cups sliced asparagus or broccoli florets.

Quick Skillet Beef Stew for One

1	each small carrot, parsnip and potato	1
3 oz	lean round or sirloin tip steak	75 g
1 tsp	vegetable oil	5 mL
1/2 tsp	Cajun spice mix	2 mL
1/3 cup	canned beef broth (undiluted)	75 mL
1/4 cup	tomato sauce	50 mL
1	small onion, quartered	1
1 tsp	all-purpose flour	5 mL
1/3 cup	frozen peas (optional)	75 mL
	Salt and pepper	

● Peel and cut carrot, parsnip and potato into bite-size chunks; set aside. Cut steak into thin strips.

● In nonstick skillet, toss steak with oil and Cajun spice; cook, stirring often, over medium-high heat until browned.

● Stir in beef broth and tomato sauce. Add onion, carrot, parsnip and potato; bring to boil. Reduce heat to medium; cover and cook, stirring occasionally, for 15 minutes or until meat is tender.

● Blend flour with 1/3 cup (75 mL) water; stir into pan along with peas (if using). Cook, stirring, for about 5 minutes or until thickened. Season with salt and pepper to taste. Makes 1 serving.

When cooking for one or two, it's hard to use up a large variety of spices and herbs before they go stale. That's why spice mixes such as this Cajun one — available where spices are sold — come in handy. Serve this hearty stew with whole wheat rolls.

TIP: Save any unused undiluted beef or chicken broth for a quick bowl of soup with the addition of noodles and sliced green onion and carrot. Or, freeze and use in other sauces, stews or soups.

Pork with Snow Peas and Couscous for One ▲

A *nice 4-ounce (125 g) boneless pork chop or pork steak makes a very quick and satisfying supper for one. The recipe doubles easily, in case you want to invite a guest.*

1/4 cup	couscous	50 mL
1 tbsp	chopped fresh parsley	15 mL
1	boneless pork chop	1
	Salt and pepper	
1 tsp	sesame or vegetable oil	5 mL
1	carrot, julienned	1
2	green onions, cut into thirds	2
1/2 cup	snow peas, trimmed	125 mL
1 tsp	minced gingerroot	5 mL
1/2 cup	canned chicken broth (undiluted)	125 mL
1 tsp	all-purpose flour	5 mL
1 tsp	lemon juice	5 mL

● In liquid measure, pour enough hot water over couscous to make 1/3 cup (75 mL); stir in parsley. Set aside.

● Trim off any fat from pork; cut horizontally into 3 slices. Sprinkle lightly with salt and pepper. In nonstick skillet, heat oil over medium-high heat; cook pork, turning once, for 2 to 3 minutes or until browned on each side. Push to side of pan.

● Add carrot, onions, snow peas and ginger; stir-fry for 1 minute. Push to side of pan.

● Combine chicken broth, flour and lemon juice; add to pan and cook, stirring, over medium heat for 1 minute or until slightly thickened. Stir vegetables and pork into sauce.

● Spoon couscous into one corner of skillet; cover and cook over low heat for about 2 minutes or just until heated through. Season with salt and pepper to taste. Makes 1 serving.

Apple Sauerkraut Pork Chops

4	pork chops	4
2 tsp	vegetable oil	10 mL
1/2 tsp	dried thyme	2 mL
	Salt and pepper	
1	pkg (19 oz/540 mL) sauerkraut (or about 1 lb/500 g)	1
1	red apple, chopped	1
1/2 tsp	caraway seeds	2 mL
1	bay leaf	1
	Red apple slices	
	Chopped fresh parsley	

● Trim off any fat from pork. In large ovenproof skillet, heat oil over medium heat; brown pork for 2 minutes on each side. Sprinkle with thyme; season with salt and pepper to taste.

● Meanwhile, drain sauerkraut; rinse under cold water and drain well. In bowl, combine sauerkraut, chopped apple, caraway seeds, bay leaf and 1/4 tsp (1 mL) pepper; spoon around and under chops in skillet.

● Bake in 350°F (180°C) oven for about 45 minutes or until chops are tender. Discard bay leaf. Garnish with apple slices and parsley. Makes 4 servings.

Bake potatoes and squash in the oven along with this easy skillet supper.

TIP: Like other ingredients, sauerkraut varies in quality. The homemade product available at markets or delis, often in plastic bags, is both tastier and milder than most canned products. All sauerkraut needs to be lightly rinsed to remove excess salt.

Quick Curried Lamb

1 tsp	vegetable oil	5 mL
2	onions, chopped	2
2	cloves garlic, minced	2
12 oz	ground lamb or beef	375 g
1 tbsp	curry powder	15 mL
1 tbsp	liquid honey	15 mL
2 tsp	chopped gingerroot	10 mL
1 tsp	ground cumin	5 mL
1/4 tsp	each ground coriander, salt and pepper	1 mL
1	carrot, sliced	1
1	sweet green pepper, cut into chunks	1
1	can (19 oz/540 mL) chick-peas, drained	1
1	can (19 oz/540 mL) tomatoes, chopped	1
1/2 cup	raisins	125 mL

● In nonstick skillet, heat oil over medium heat; cook onions and garlic, stirring occasionally, for 3 minutes or until softened.

● Add lamb; cook, stirring to break up meat, for about 5 minutes or until no longer pink. Skim off fat. Stir in curry powder, honey, ginger, cumin, coriander, salt and pepper.

● Stir in carrot, green pepper, chick-peas, tomatoes and raisins; bring to boil. Reduce heat to low; cook, stirring occasionally, for 20 minutes or until thickened slightly and vegetables are tender. Makes 4 servings.

This ground lamb curry is so speedy that you'll need to start the rice first. Pair it with sliced cucumbers and radishes dressed with plain yogurt and chopped fresh mint.

Paella ▶

Paella, which originates in the rice-growing districts of southern Spain, is basically rice and vegetables with embellishments. This chicken, sausage and shrimp version is a good one to serve when you're looking for an impressive entertaining dish. If you prefer to use clams, they'll need a scrub under cold running water.

12	mussels or clams	12
1/4 cup	all-purpose flour	50 mL
Pinch	each salt and pepper	Pinch
2-1/2 lb	chicken pieces	1.25 kg
1/4 cup	olive oil	50 mL
1 cup	chopped onions	250 mL
2	cloves garlic, minced	2
1/2 tsp	saffron threads (or 1/4 tsp/1 mL saffron powder)	2 mL
1 cup	hot chicken stock	250 mL
1	can (28 oz/796 mL) tomatoes	1
1/2 tsp	dried oregano	2 mL
1 cup	long grain rice	250 mL
1 lb	raw shrimp, peeled and deveined (see p. 42)	500 g
2 cups	frozen peas	500 mL
	Lemon wedges and pimiento strips	

● Scrub mussels under running water and remove any beards; discard any that do not close when tapped. Set aside.

● In shallow dish, combine flour, salt and pepper; toss chicken in mixture to coat lightly.

● In large deep skillet, heat oil over medium-high heat; brown chicken for about 5 minutes on each side. Remove and set aside.

● Drain off all but 3 tbsp (50 mL) fat from pan. Reduce heat to medium. Add onions and garlic; cook, stirring occasionally, for 3 to 5 minutes or until softened. Dissolve saffron in stock; add to pan. Stir in tomatoes and oregano; bring to boil. Stir in rice. Return chicken to pan.

● Reduce heat to low. Cover and cook for 30 minutes or until juices run clear when chicken is pierced. Nestle shrimp and mussels into rice; cover and cook for 10 to 15 minutes or until liquid is absorbed and mussels have opened. Discard any mussels that do not open.

● Stir in peas; cover and let stand for 1 minute or until heated through. Garnish with lemon and pimiento. Makes 8 servings.

TIP: Saffron is more expensive than gold, but worth every penny you pay for its burnished glow and the special flavor it gives to rice. If possible, always buy saffron in strands rather than powdered, where flavor is lost.

Hoisin Fish and Vegetable Medley

Monkfish, shark, salmon, halibut and ocean perch are all firm enough to withstand stir-frying. Serve over rice.

1 lb	frozen fish fillets, thawed	500 g
2 tbsp	mirin (rice wine)	25 mL
1 tbsp	hoisin sauce	15 mL
1 tbsp	soy sauce	15 mL
1 tbsp	sesame oil	15 mL
2	carrots, julienned	2
1 cup	snow peas, trimmed	250 mL
1/2 cup	sliced mushrooms	125 mL

● Cut fish into 1-inch (2.5 cm) pieces. In small dish, mix together mirin, hoisin sauce and soy sauce; set aside.

● Heat wok or large skillet over medium heat; add oil, swirling to coat pan. Stir-fry carrots, snow peas and mushrooms for 2 minutes. Add fish; gently stir-fry for 1 minute.

● Stir in mirin mixture; cover and cook, stirring occasionally, for 3 to 4 minutes or until fish is opaque. Makes 4 servings.

STIR-FRY BASICS

● The typical rounded-bottom wok works fine in Chinese restaurants where very hot gas flames lick up the sides of the pan. For home use, however, a flat-bottomed wok that sits firmly on the burner gets the most heat to the food in the shortest possible time. If you don't have a wok, use a deep skillet or shallow Dutch oven for equally good results.

● Cut the ingredients for any stir-fry to a uniform size to ensure even cooking. Then, set the bowls by the wok in the order of use.

● Always heat the empty wok over high heat until a drop of water sizzles on the surface before adding the oil and swirling it over the bottom and up the side of the pan.

● To stir-fry, place lifter under ingredients, then lift and toss gently. Avoid aggressive stirring, especially as ingredients soften.

Shrimp Vegetable Stir-Fry

T*his is a quick-from-scratch supper, especially if you buy shrimp that's already peeled and deveined.*

1 tbsp	vegetable oil	15 mL
1	clove garlic, minced	1
1 tbsp	minced gingerroot	15 mL
1 lb	raw shrimp, peeled and deveined	500 g
4 cups	broccoli florets	1 L
1	sweet red pepper, sliced	1
1	large carrot, thinly sliced	1
1/4 cup	water	50 mL
2 cups	bean sprouts	500 mL
1	can (8 oz/227 g) sliced water chestnuts, drained	1
	SAUCE	
1/3 cup	oyster sauce	75 mL
3 tbsp	pineapple juice	45 mL
1 tbsp	cornstarch	15 mL

1 tbsp	soy sauce	15 mL
1 tbsp	rice vinegar	15 mL
1-1/2 tsp	liquid honey	7 mL
1-1/2 tsp	sesame oil	7 mL
1/4 tsp	hot pepper sauce	1 mL

● SAUCE: Whisk together oyster sauce, pineapple juice, cornstarch, soy sauce, vinegar, honey, sesame oil and hot pepper sauce; set aside.

● Heat wok or large skillet over high heat; add oil, swirling to coat pan. Stir-fry garlic and ginger for 30 seconds. Add shrimp; stir-fry for 2 minutes. Add broccoli, red pepper and carrot; stir-fry for 1 minute. Add water; cover and steam for 5 minutes or until vegetables are tender-crisp. Push to side of pan.

● Stir sauce mixture; add to wok and cook, stirring, for about 1 minute or until thickened. Stir shrimp mixture into sauce until coated. Stir in bean sprouts and water chestnuts. Makes 4 servings.

TIP: Double the sauce to have extra on hand for stir-frying with chicken or vegetables. It keeps for up to one week in the refrigerator.

PEELING SHRIMP

The larger the shrimp, the more they cost. That's simply because the large ones are faster to peel and devein. This task is not hard, just tedious if you have a lot.

● To prepare shrimp, start at the thick end, peeling off rounds of shell until you reach the last tail segment, which you can leave on or take off. Using a sharp paring knife, make a shallow cut along the center of the rounded back and pull out the dark vein.

Chicken and Scallop Pad Thai ▼

8 oz	rice stick noodles	250 g
1/2 cup	chili sauce	125 mL
1/4 cup	fish sauce	50 mL
2 tbsp	each rice wine vinegar and lemon juice	25 mL
1 lb	boneless skinless chicken breasts	500 g
1 tbsp	cornstarch	15 mL
3 tbsp	(approx) vegetable oil	45 mL
1 tsp	sesame oil	5 mL
6	cloves garlic, minced	6
6	green onions, chopped	6
1	each small sweet green and red pepper, sliced	1
8 oz	scallops, cut in half	250 g
3/4 tsp	hot pepper flakes	4 mL
1	egg, lightly beaten	1
2 cups	bean sprouts	500 mL
6	green onions, sliced	6
1/4 cup	chopped fresh coriander	50 mL
	Toasted almonds or cashews	
	Coriander sprigs and lime wedges	

● In large bowl, soak noodles in warm water for 15 minutes; drain and place in large bowl. Set aside.

● Meanwhile, mix together chili sauce, fish sauce, vinegar and lemon juice; set aside. Cut chicken into strips; toss with cornstarch. Set aside.

● Heat large skillet over medium-high heat; add 1 tbsp (15 mL) of the vegetable oil and sesame oil, swirling to coat pan. Stir-fry garlic and chopped onions for 3 minutes or until softened. Add green and red peppers; stir-fry for 2 to 3 minutes or until starting to soften. Add to noodles in bowl.

● Add 1 tbsp (15 mL) of the remaining oil to pan; stir-fry chicken for 5 to 8 minutes

or until browned and no longer pink inside. Add scallops, and remaining oil if necessary; cook, turning, for 2 to 3 minutes or until opaque.

● Add hot pepper flakes and fish sauce mixture; bring to boil. Reduce heat to medium. Stir in egg; cook, stirring, for about 1 minute or until sauce has thickened. Add to noodle mixture.

● Add bean sprouts, sliced onions and coriander; toss together. Garnish with almonds, coriander sprigs and lime wedges. Makes 8 servings.

Fish sauce, as common in Southeast Asian countries as soy sauce is in China, is indispensable to the taste of this popular dish. Look for the brand with the squid on the label and store in the refrigerator once opened.

Herbed Vegetables with Eggs and Toast ▼

A *wok or skillet does it all —
toasts the bread, scrambles
the eggs and whips up the
vegetable accompaniment.
This is a deliciously quick
meal for small households or
fledgling cooks.*

2	thick slices crusty bread	2
1 tbsp	vegetable oil	15 mL
3	eggs, beaten	3
1	onion, coarsely chopped	1
1	clove garlic, minced	1
1/4 cup	chicken stock	50 mL
1	large zucchini, cut into chunks	1
1	tomato, coarsely chopped	1
1/2 tsp	Italian dried herb seasoning	2 mL
	Salt and pepper	

● Brush both sides of bread with half of the oil; cut in half and set aside.

● Heat wok or large skillet over high heat; add remaining oil, swirling to coat pan. Pour in eggs; cook, lifting eggs to let uncooked portion flow underneath, for 30 to 45 seconds or until set but still moist. Spoon onto plate; invert another plate on top to keep warm.

● Add bread to wok; cook, turning, over medium-high heat for 2 minutes or until toasted. Remove and set aside.

● Add onion and garlic to wok; stir-fry for 2 minutes, adding a little of the stock, if needed, to prevent sticking. Stir in remaining stock, zucchini, tomato and Italian seasoning; cook, stirring occasionally, for 5 minutes or just until zucchini is tender. Season with salt and pepper to taste. Serve over eggs on toast. Makes 2 servings.

Tofu Vegetable Stir-Fry

2	stalks celery	2
12 oz	extra-firm tofu	375 g
1/4 cup	hoisin sauce	50 mL
3 tbsp	soy sauce	45 mL
1 tbsp	liquid honey	15 mL
3 tbsp	vegetable oil	45 mL
2	cloves garlic, minced	2
1 tbsp	chopped gingerroot	15 mL
3	green onions, chopped	3
2	carrots, thinly sliced	2
2	sweet green peppers, cut into chunks	2
1	onion, cut into chunks	1
1/2 cup	chicken stock	125 mL
1/2 tsp	chili paste	2 mL
1 tbsp	cornstarch	15 mL
1 tbsp	sesame oil	15 mL
2 tbsp	chopped fresh coriander or parsley	25 mL

● Cut celery into 1-inch (2.5 cm) pieces; set aside.

● Cut tofu into 1-inch (2.5 cm) chunks; pat dry. In bowl, combine 2 tbsp (25 mL) of the hoisin sauce, 1 tbsp (15 mL) of the soy sauce and honey. Add tofu; stir to coat.

● Heat large skillet or wok over high heat; add 1 tbsp (15 mL) of the vegetable oil, swirling to coat pan. Drain tofu; stir-fry for about 5 minutes or until browned. Remove and set aside.

● Add remaining vegetable oil to skillet; stir-fry garlic, ginger and green onions for 30 seconds. Add reserved celery, carrots, green peppers and onion; stir-fry for 5 minutes.

● Stir together chicken stock, chili paste and remaining hoisin and soy sauces; add to skillet and bring to boil. Add tofu; reduce heat and simmer for 5 minutes.

● Combine cornstarch, 2 tbsp (25 mL) water and sesame oil; add to skillet and cook, stirring, for 1 minute or until thickened. Sprinkle with coriander. Makes 4 servings.

Extra-firm tofu is our pick for stir-frying. It soaks up the spicy hoisin sauce like a sponge and doesn't crumble or mush like softer regular tofu. Serve over big bowls of steaming rice.

Rösti with Cheese and Spinach

4 cups	packed fresh spinach	1 L
3	large baking potatoes, peeled	3
Pinch	nutmeg	Pinch
	Salt and pepper	
2 tbsp	butter	25 mL
1	small onion, chopped	1
1	cup shredded Cheddar cheese	250 mL

● Rinse spinach; shake off excess water. In saucepan, cook spinach, with just the water clinging to leaves, over high heat for 1 to 2 minutes or until wilted. Drain and let cool slightly; squeeze out liquid and chop coarsely. Set aside.

● In saucepan of boiling water, cook potatoes for 10 minutes; drain and let cool. Grate into bowl; stir in nutmeg, and salt and pepper to taste.

● In 9-inch (23 cm) nonstick skillet, melt half of the butter over medium heat; cook onion, stirring occasionally, for 2 to 3 minutes or until softened. Remove and set aside.

● Pat half of the potato mixture evenly over bottom of skillet. Spread spinach over top, without touching side of skillet. Top with onion and cheese, without touching side of skillet. Cover with remaining potato mixture, pressing at edges to seal. Cook over medium heat for 10 minutes.

● Invert onto flat dinner plate. Add remaining butter to skillet; slide potato cake back into skillet, browned side up. Cook for 8 to 10 minutes longer or until browned on bottom. Slide out onto serving plate. Tent with foil and let stand for 5 minutes before cutting. Makes 4 servings.

This skillet-sized potato pancake is especially tasty with spinach tucked inside. Serve in wedges and add muesli rolls and sliced tomatoes and cucumbers tossed with oil and vinegar.

Light Pasta Primavera ▶

Springtime vegetables simmered in a light cream sauce coat fusilli to perfection. Fresh basil adds the herb high notes. Crusty rolls and a colorful tomato salad round out the menu.

1 lb	asparagus (see TIP below)	500 g
1 tbsp	butter	15 mL
1	onion, chopped	1
2	cloves garlic, minced	2
3 cups	sliced mushrooms (about 8 oz/250 g)	750 mL
2	carrots, sliced	2
1	large zucchini, chopped	1
1/2 cup	chopped fresh basil	125 mL
3/4 tsp	salt	4 mL
1/2 tsp	pepper	2 mL
2 tbsp	all-purpose flour	25 mL
1	can (385 mL) 2% evaporated milk	1
4 cups	fusilli	1 L
1/3 cup	freshly grated Parmesan cheese	75 mL

● Trim asparagus; reserve bases for another use. Cut stalks into 1-1/2-inch (4 cm) pieces. Set aside.

● In nonstick skillet, melt butter over medium-high heat; cook onion, garlic and mushrooms, stirring occasionally, for 5 minutes.

● Stir in carrots, zucchini, asparagus, 2 tbsp (25 mL) of the basil, 2 tbsp (25 mL) water, salt and pepper; cover and cook over medium heat for 5 minutes. Uncover and cook for 1 to 2 minutes or until almost all liquid has evaporated.

● Stir in flour; cook, stirring, for 1 minute. Pour in milk; cook, stirring, for 5 minutes or until thickened.

● Meanwhile, in large pot of boiling salted water, cook fusilli for 8 to 10 minutes or until tender but firm; drain and toss with sauce. Sprinkle with Parmesan and remaining basil; toss again. Makes 4 servings.

TIP: To trim asparagus, hold each stalk at center and base. Bend until stalk snaps at natural breaking point. Save ends to make an easy spring soup — simply simmer them in chicken stock with a diced potato and onion, then pass through a food mill to purée, extracting coarse fibers.

Broccoli and Shrimp Pasta for One

One pot is all you need to cook up pasta, a goodly portion of healthful broccoli and enough shrimp to make the dish feel special.

1	bunch broccoli	1
3/4 cup	rotini	175 mL
1/2 cup	cooked salad shrimp	125 mL
1	green onion, chopped	1
1 tsp	butter	5 mL
1 tsp	lemon juice	5 mL
	Salt and pepper	
2 tbsp	freshly grated Parmesan cheese	25 mL

● Cut broccoli into small florets; reserve stalks for another use.

● In large pot of boiling salted water, cook rotini for 6 minutes. Add broccoli; cook for 2 minutes or until pasta is tender but firm. Drain off all but 2 tbsp (25 mL) liquid.

● Reduce heat to low. Stir in shrimp, onion, butter, lemon juice, and salt and pepper to taste; toss gently. Sprinkle with Parmesan. Makes 1 serving.

Simmering Stews

No-tend stews make for extra-easy cooking. Once the medley of roots, herbs and meat or chicken is in the pot, gentle simmering allows the rich flavors to mellow and blend to tasty perfection.

All-New Oven Stew ▶

This delicious nineties-style stew does away with the messy browning of meat and contains less fat than most old-fashioned versions.

4	large carrots	4
2	stalks celery	2
Half	small rutabaga, peeled	Half
1-1/2 lb	cross rib or blade steak, 1-1/2 inches (4 cm) thick	750 g
1 tbsp	vegetable oil	15 mL
3	onions, quartered	3
2	large cloves garlic, minced	2
1/2 tsp	each dried thyme and marjoram	2 mL
1/4 cup	all-purpose flour	50 mL
1 cup	beef stock	250 mL
1 cup	dry red wine or beef stock	250 mL
1	can (19 oz/540 mL) tomatoes	1
3	large potatoes, peeled and cut into chunks	3
1 cup	frozen peas	250 mL
	Salt and pepper	
2 tbsp	chopped fresh parsley	25 mL

● Cut carrots, celery and rutabaga into 2-inch (5 cm) chunks.

● Trim off any fat from steak. Slice steak into 1-1/2-inch (4 cm) wide strips; cut crosswise into 1-1/2-inch (4 cm) cubes.

● In large Dutch oven, heat oil over medium heat; cook onions, stirring occasionally, for about 5 minutes or until lightly colored. Add garlic, thyme and marjoram; cook, stirring, for 1 minute.

● Add beef, carrots, celery and rutabaga; sprinkle with flour and cook, stirring, for about 1 minute or until flour is well moistened.

● Stir in stock, wine and tomatoes, breaking up tomatoes with back of spoon; bring to boil. Cover and bake in 325°F (160°C) oven for 1-1/2 hours.

● Stir in potatoes; cover and bake, stirring once, for about 1-1/4 hours or until meat and potatoes are fork-tender. Stir in peas; cook for about 2 minutes or until heated through. Season with salt and pepper to taste. Sprinkle with parsley. Makes 8 servings.

VARIATION

● CURRIED BEEF STEW: Substitute 1 tbsp (15 mL) finely chopped gingerroot, 4 tsp (20 mL) curry powder and 1 tsp (5 mL) each ground cumin and coriander for thyme and marjoram; cook along with garlic. Instead of rutabaga, cut half a cauliflower into florets; add for last 20 minutes of baking.

TIP: To make stew ahead of time, bake for the first 1-1/2 hours, then cool and freeze for up to 2 weeks. Thaw in refrigerator and proceed with recipe, baking for about 15 minutes longer.

Burgundy Beef ▲

Here's a stew to stash in your freezer for make-ahead entertaining. Spooning it into a Parsleyed Rice Ring (see box, next page) doesn't take much time, and makes it look all the more impressive and special.

2 lb	lean stewing beef	1 kg
3 tbsp	all-purpose flour	50 mL
1/2 tsp	salt	2 mL
1/4 tsp	pepper	1 mL
2 tbsp	(approx) vegetable oil	25 mL
3	carrots, chopped	3
2	cloves garlic, minced	2
1	onion, chopped	1
1 cup	beef stock	250 mL
3/4 cup	dry red wine or beef stock	175 mL
2	bay leaves	2
1/2 tsp	dried thyme	2 mL
1 lb	small mushrooms	500 g
16	pearl onions	16
1/4 cup	chopped fresh dill (optional)	50 mL

● Cut beef into 3/4-inch (2 cm) cubes, trimming off any fat. Toss with flour, salt and pepper. In large Dutch oven, heat half of the oil over high heat; brown beef, in batches and adding some of the oil if needed. Remove and set aside.

● Add remaining oil to pan; cook carrots, garlic and chopped onion, stirring occasionally, for about 3 minutes or until onion is softened.

● Return beef to pan. Add stock, wine, bay leaves and thyme; bring to boil, stirring to scrape up brown bits. Reduce heat, cover and simmer for 1 hour.

● Add mushrooms and pearl onions; cover and simmer for 30 minutes or until tender. Discard bay leaves. *(Stew can be cooled in refrigerator and stored in airtight container for up to 2 days or frozen for up to 4 weeks.)* Sprinkle with dill (if using). Makes 8 servings.

PEELING PEARL ONIONS

Pearl onions, abundant in the early fall and treasures for any stew, are time-consuming to peel. To slip the papery covering off mini onions, cover onions with boiling water for about 2 minutes. Drain, cool under cold water and drain again. This blanching makes the onions easier to peel.

Daube of Beef with Orange

3 lb	lean stewing beef	1.5 kg
1	large orange	1
1-1/2 cups	dry red wine	375 mL
2 tbsp	olive oil	25 mL
1 tsp	each salt and dried thyme	5 mL
1/2 tsp	pepper	2 mL
1	bay leaf	1
3	cloves garlic, crushed	3
8 oz	bacon	250 g
3 cups	small mushrooms (8 oz/250 g)	750 g
8	carrots, sliced	8
16	pearl onions (or 4 small onions, quartered)	16
1/2 cup	all-purpose flour	125 mL
2-1/2 cups	beef stock	625 mL
2 tbsp	tomato paste	25 mL

● Cut beef into 2-inch (5 cm) cubes, trimming off any fat. Cut long 1/2-inch (1 cm) wide strip of rind from orange. In large bowl, combine beef, orange rind, wine, oil, salt, thyme, pepper, bay leaf and garlic; cover and marinate in refrigerator for at least 6 hours or up to 24 hours.

● Cut bacon into 2-inch (5 cm) pieces; arrange one-third over bottom of 20- or 24-cup (5 or 6 L) casserole. Cover with half of the mushrooms, half of the carrots and half of the onions.

● With slotted spoon, remove beef from marinade; toss with flour to coat completely. Arrange half over vegetables. Repeat layers; cover with remaining bacon.

● Stir stock and tomato paste into marinade in bowl; pour over casserole. Cover and bake in 325°F (160°C) oven, stirring twice, for 3-1/2 to 4 hours or until beef is tender. Discard bay leaf and orange rind. *(Stew can be cooled in refrigerator and stored in airtight container for up to 2 days; let stand at room temperature for 30 minutes before reheating.)* Makes 8 servings.

TIP: If desired, replace the wine with 1 cup (250 mL) beef stock and 1/4 cup (50 mL) each red wine vinegar and orange juice. The latter adds extra zing and harmonizes beautifully with the orange rind already in the stew.

REPLACING WINE IN A STEW
When replacing wine in a stew, an unsalted stock (chicken, beef or vegetable) is often the best choice. However, unless you make your own, the choice from among cubes, powdered and canned stocks can produce a very salty stew. Be sure to eliminate any other addition of salt in the recipe — you can always taste and adjust the seasoning just before serving. Then replace about 1 tbsp (15 mL) of each cup (250 mL) stock with red or white wine vinegar or cider vinegar.

*W*ith a bounty of button mushrooms and pearl onions, this layered stew from southern France is grand enough for company. It's absolutely delicious with garlic mashed potatoes or a short pasta such as rotini, and something green and crisp — salad, asparagus, sugar snap peas or fresh beans.

Polenta with Beef and Sausage Ragout ▶

Here's stew Italian-style, with your choice of mild or spicy sausage. One pound (500 g) of short pasta such as rotini or conchiglie (shells) can replace the polenta.

2 tbsp	olive oil	25 mL
2	onions, chopped	2
3	cloves garlic, finely chopped	3
1/4 tsp	hot pepper flakes	1 mL
8 oz	Italian sausage	250 g
1-1/2 lb	lean ground beef	750 g
4 cups	sliced mushrooms (12 oz/375 g)	1 L
2	cans (each 28 oz/796 mL) tomatoes, puréed	2
	Salt and pepper	
	Polenta (recipe follows)	
1 cup	freshly grated Parmesan cheese	250 mL
1/4 cup	chopped fresh parsley	50 mL

● In large skillet, heat oil over medium heat; cook onions, garlic and hot pepper flakes, stirring occasionally, for 5 minutes or until softened.

● Remove sausage from casings; add to pan along with beef. Cook over medium-high heat, breaking up chunks with back of spoon, for 7 minutes or until browned. Skim off fat.

● Add mushrooms; cook for 5 minutes. Add tomatoes and bring to boil; reduce heat and simmer for 30 minutes or until thickened. Season with salt and pepper to taste.

● Spoon Polenta into individual bowls; top with ragout. Sprinkle with Parmesan and parsley. Makes 8 servings.

POLENTA		
8 cups	water	2 L
2 tsp	salt	10 mL
1/2 tsp	pepper	2 mL
2 cups	cornmeal	500 mL
1/4 cup	butter	50 mL

● In saucepan, bring water, salt and pepper to boil over high heat; gradually whisk in cornmeal until evenly thickened. Reduce heat to low; cook, stirring often with wooden spoon, for 25 to 30 minutes or until smooth and thick enough to mound stiffly on spoon. Stir in butter. Makes 8 servings.

Meatballs in Sweet and Sour Sauce

This delicious recipe proves that, even on a tight schedule, it's possible to make meatballs and have them on the table in less than 30 minutes. Serve with rice and broccoli florets.

1	egg	1
1/4 cup	dry bread crumbs	50 mL
3/4 tsp	salt	4 mL
1/2 tsp	pepper	2 mL
1 lb	lean ground beef	500 g
2 tsp	vegetable oil	10 mL
2	carrots, chopped	2
1	onion, chopped	1
1-3/4 cups	beef stock	425 mL
3 tbsp	cider vinegar	50 mL
1 tbsp	packed brown sugar	15 mL
1/4 tsp	each ground allspice and cloves	1 mL
1/3 cup	crushed gingersnap cookies	75 mL
1 tbsp	chopped fresh parsley	15 mL

● In bowl, beat egg; mix in bread crumbs, salt and pepper. Mix in beef; shape into 1-1/2-inch (4 cm) balls.

● In large nonstick skillet, heat oil over medium-high heat; brown meatballs, turning occasionally, for about 5 minutes. Drain off fat.

● Add carrots and onion; cook, stirring often, for about 3 minutes or until softened. Stir in beef stock, vinegar, sugar, allspice and cloves; bring to boil. Reduce heat, cover and simmer for 15 minutes or until meatballs are no longer pink inside.

● Add gingersnap crumbs; simmer, stirring, for 5 minutes or until thickened. Sprinkle with parsley. Makes 4 servings.

Orange Teriyaki Roast Pork

Since nothing is easier to prepare for a weekend meal than a roast, why not add parboiled cabbage wedges to the roasting pan and transform this economical cut of pork into a satisfying one-dish meal.

3 lb	pork butt roast	1.5 kg
1/4 cup	orange juice	50 mL
1/4 cup	soy sauce	50 mL
1 tbsp	granulated sugar	15 mL
1 tbsp	grated orange rind	15 mL
1 tbsp	minced gingerroot (or 1/2 tsp/2 mL ground ginger)	15 mL
2	cloves garlic, minced	2
1/2 tsp	pepper	2 mL
1	small savoy cabbage	1

● Place pork in sturdy plastic bag; set in bowl. Combine orange juice, soy sauce, sugar, orange rind, ginger, garlic and pepper; pour over roast. Seal and marinate in refrigerator for at least 2 hours or up to 6 hours. Let stand at room temperature for 30 minutes.

● Reserving marinade, place roast on rack in shallow roasting pan. Roast in 325°F (160°C) oven, basting occasionally with marinade, for 1-1/2 hours.

● Meanwhile, cut cabbage into wedges. In saucepan of boiling water, cook cabbage for 5 minutes; drain and arrange around roast on rack.

● Roast, turning cabbage once and basting cabbage and roast, for 30 to 45 minutes longer or until meat thermometer registers 160°F (70°C) and cabbage is tender.

● Keeping cabbage warm, remove roast to carving board and tent with foil; let stand for 10 minutes before carving. Serve with cabbage wedges. Makes 8 servings.

Roast Lamb with Potatoes

A succulent leg of lamb roasted to tender perfection on a bed of potatoes suits any special occasion. Just add a salad and you're set.

4 lb	bone-in leg of lamb	2 kg
3	cloves garlic, slivered	3
2 tbsp	liquid honey	25 mL
1 tbsp	chopped fresh rosemary (or 1/2 tsp/2 mL dried)	15 mL
1 tbsp	Dijon mustard	15 mL
1 tsp	salt	5 mL
1/2 tsp	pepper	2 mL
1/2 cup	water or chicken stock	125 mL
	POTATOES	
7	baking potatoes (3 lb/1.5 kg)	7
2 tbsp	olive oil	25 mL
1 tsp	chopped fresh rosemary (or pinch dried)	5 mL
1 tsp	salt	5 mL
1/2 tsp	pepper	2 mL
1	clove garlic, minced	1

● Trim off any fat from lamb; cut little slits in meaty portions and insert garlic slivers. Combine honey, rosemary, mustard, salt and pepper; brush over lamb.

● POTATOES: Peel and slice potatoes thinly; place in 13- x 9-inch (3 L) baking dish. Combine oil, rosemary, salt, pepper and garlic; toss with potatoes. Spread potatoes over bottom of dish; place lamb on top.

● Pour water over potatoes. Roast in 425°F (220°C) oven for 15 minutes. Reduce heat to 350°F (180°C); roast for 50 to 60 minutes or until lamb is rare to medium-rare and meat thermometer registers 140°F to 150°F (60°C to 65°C).

● Keeping potatoes warm, transfer lamb to platter and tent with foil; let stand for 10 minutes before carving. Serve with potatoes. Makes 6 servings.

Pork Chili with Squash and Beans

2-1/2 lb	boneless pork shoulder or butt	1.25 kg
3 tbsp	(approx) vegetable oil	50 mL
4	onions, chopped	4
4	cloves garlic, minced	4
1	sweet green pepper, diced	1
1 tbsp	minced fresh or pickled jalapeño pepper (or 1/2 tsp/2 mL hot pepper flakes)	15 mL
2 tbsp	chili powder	25 mL
2 tsp	dried oregano	10 mL
1-1/2 tsp	ground cumin	7 mL
2	cans (each 19 oz/540 mL) tomatoes	2
1	butternut squash (2 lb/1 kg)	1
3	cans (each 19 oz/540 mL) romano or kidney beans, drained and rinsed	3
	Salt and pepper	

● Cut pork into bite-size cubes, trimming off any fat. In large Dutch oven, heat 1 tbsp (15 mL) of the oil over medium-high heat; brown pork, in batches and adding oil as needed. Remove and set aside.

● Reduce heat to medium. If needed, add remaining oil to pan; cook onions, garlic and green pepper, stirring occasionally, for 3 minutes or until softened. Stir in jalapeño pepper, chili powder, oregano and cumin; cook, stirring, for 2 minutes.

● Add tomatoes, breaking up with back of spoon. Return pork to pan; bring to boil, stirring to scrape up brown bits. Reduce heat, cover and simmer, stirring occasionally, for 1 hour.

● Meanwhile, halve, seed and peel squash; cut into bite-size pieces. Add to pan along with beans; cover and simmer for 20 to 30 minutes or until pork and squash are tender. Season with salt and pepper to taste. Makes 8 servings.

Nutritious squash adds flavor and color to a satisfying chili stew.

TIP: Because butternut squash is easier to peel and cut than other winter squashes, it gets our nod for cubing and simmering in chilis and stews. Substitute nutrient-dense sweet potatoes, if desired, or the winter squash of your choice.

RESCUING A WATERY STEW

What to do when the stew is cooked, the meat and vegetables are tender — but there's just too much juice? Simply boiling the stew with the top off until it thickens will certainly overcook the vegetables. Try one of these chef's tricks instead:

● Pour the stew into a colander set over a large wide saucepan, reserving the contents of the colander and returning the liquid to the stove to boil over high heat until thicker and reduced enough to coat the meat and vegetables nicely.

● Blend together flour and soft butter in equal quantities; gradually stir this mixture, called "beurre manié," into the stew, stirring constantly until liquid has thickened.

● Shake up flour or cornstarch with 3 times the amount of water and pour into the stew, stirring constantly until liquid has thickened.

Braised Lamb Shanks with Beans ▶

A medley of onions, garlic, carrots, parsnips, rutabaga and beans livens up a robust lamb stew. Crusty Portuguese or Italian bread is a must to mop up the juices.

6	lamb shanks (about 4 lb/2 kg)	6
1 tbsp	vegetable oil	15 mL
4	large onions, sliced lengthwise	4
4	cloves garlic, minced	4
1	can (28 oz/796 mL) tomatoes	1
2 cups	water	500 mL
1 cup	dry red wine or beef stock	250 mL
2 tsp	crushed dried rosemary	10 mL
1 tsp	salt	5 mL
3/4 tsp	dried thyme	4 mL
1/2 tsp	pepper	2 mL
2	bay leaves	2
4	carrots, cubed	4
2	parsnips, peeled and cubed	2
Half	rutabaga, peeled and cubed	Half
1	can (19 oz/540 mL) white kidney beans, drained and rinsed	1
1/4 cup	chopped fresh parsley	50 mL

● Trim off any fat from lamb. In large Dutch oven, heat oil over medium-high heat; brown lamb all over, in batches if necessary. Remove and set aside.

● Drain off fat from pan. Reduce heat to medium. Add onions and garlic; cook, stirring occasionally, for 8 minutes or until tender.

● Return lamb to pan. Add tomatoes, breaking up with back of spoon. Add water, wine, rosemary, salt, thyme, pepper and bay leaves; bring to boil. Reduce heat to low, cover and simmer for 1 hour. Add carrots, parsnips and rutabaga; cover and simmer for 40 minutes or until vegetables are tender.

● Using slotted spoon, transfer meat and vegetables to serving platter; keep warm.

● Discard bay leaves. Skim off fat from pan juices; boil for 10 minutes or until thickened slightly. Add beans and heat through. Pour over meat and vegetables; sprinkle with parsley. Makes 6 servings.

Spicy Lamb Stew

Add the yogurt in this Indian-style stew a spoonful at a time to prevent it from curdling.

1 tbsp	vegetable oil	15 mL
1-1/2 lb	boneless lamb, trimmed and cut into 1-inch (2.5 cm) cubes	750 g
2	large onions, chopped	2
2	carrots, chopped	2
2	cloves garlic, minced	2
1 tbsp	minced gingerroot	15 mL
1/2 cup	plain yogurt	125 mL
1 tsp	each ground cumin and coriander	5 mL
1/2 tsp	cinnamon	2 mL
Pinch	cayenne pepper	Pinch
1	tomato, chopped	1
1/2 cup	chicken stock	125 mL
	Salt and pepper	
1/4 cup	chopped fresh coriander or parsley	50 mL

● In large Dutch oven, heat oil over high heat; brown lamb, in batches if necessary. Remove and set aside.

● Drain off any fat from pan. Reduce heat to medium. Add onions, carrots, garlic and ginger; cook, stirring occasionally, for 2 minutes or until softened. Stir in yogurt, 1 tbsp (15 mL) at a time; add cumin, coriander, cinnamon and cayenne.

● Return lamb to pan. Add tomato and stock; cover and simmer for 1-1/2 hours. Uncover and simmer for 20 minutes or until lamb is tender. Season with salt and pepper to taste. Sprinkle with coriander. Makes 4 servings.

New Orleans Hands-On Supper ▶

Down in Louisiana's "Big Easy," this bib-and-fingers supper consists of potatoes, corn, crawfish and hot-as-Hades spicy sausage. Up here, shrimp takes over from Gulf crawfish — but covering the table with newspapers, rolling up your sleeves and using your hands to enjoy the feast is just as authentic.

2 lb	small new red potatoes (about 18)	1 kg
4	cobs of corn, husked	4
1 lb	raw jumbo shrimp	500 g
2 lb	hot Italian sausage	1 kg
1 lb	green beans, trimmed	500 g
	SPICE MIXTURE	
1 tbsp	mustard seeds	15 mL
1 tsp	salt	5 mL
1	bay leaf	1
1/2 tsp	each ground ginger, whole cloves, whole allspice and black peppercorns	2 mL
1/4 tsp	hot pepper flakes	1 mL

● SPICE MIXTURE: In small spice mill or blender, coarsely grind together mustard seeds, salt, bay leaf, ginger, cloves, allspice, peppercorns and hot pepper flakes.

● In large stockpot, bring 12 cups (3 L) water and spice mixture to boil; reduce heat and simmer for 5 minutes.

● Meanwhile, scrub potatoes. Cut each corn cob into 4 pieces. Using scissors, cut through shell along back of each shrimp; remove vein.

● Add potatoes and sausage to pot; simmer for 15 minutes. Add corn and beans; simmer for 3 to 4 minutes or until beans are tender-crisp. Scatter shrimp over top; cover and cook for 2 to 3 minutes or until shrimp are pink.

● Remove sausage and cut into large pieces; arrange around edge of serving platter.

● Remove and reserve 1/2 cup (125 mL) of the cooking liquid. Drain vegetable mixture in colander; arrange in center of platter. Drizzle with reserved liquid. Makes 8 servings.

Chowder-Style Mussels

Mussels are one bowlful of deliciousness. Add whole wheat rolls — split, brushed with olive oil, sprinkled with basil and toasted — plus a salad that includes peppery arugula and watercress.

2 tbsp	olive oil	25 mL
2	cloves garlic, minced	2
1	each onion, carrot and stalk celery, chopped	1
1	sweet green or yellow pepper, chopped	1
1	zucchini, diced	1
1	can (28 oz/796 mL) stewed tomatoes	1
1	bottle (237 mL) clam juice (or 1 cup/250 mL fish stock)	1
1 tsp	dried basil	5 mL
1/2 tsp	fennel seeds, crushed	2 mL
1/4 tsp	each dried thyme, cayenne and black pepper	1 mL
1-1/2 lb	mussels	750 g
1/3 cup	each chopped green onions and fresh parsley	75 mL

● In large saucepan, heat oil over medium heat; cook garlic, onion, carrot and celery, stirring often, for 5 minutes. Add green pepper and zucchini; cook for 5 minutes.

● Add tomatoes, clam juice, basil, fennel seeds, thyme, cayenne and black pepper; bring to boil, stirring. Reduce heat and simmer for 20 minutes or until thickened.

● Meanwhile, scrub mussels under running water, removing any beards. Discard any that do not close when tapped. Add to pan; cover and cook for 5 minutes or until mussels open, discarding any that do not open.

● Ladle chowder into shallow soup bowls; sprinkle with green onions and parsley. Makes 4 servings.

Lentil Pepper Ragout on Herbed Couscous

A chopped tomato and a squeeze of fresh lemon juice add color and flavor to this satisfying vegetarian stew. Keep the recipe for the couscous handy when you need a quick starch side dish. Couscous, dressed up with herbs, goes with just about any kind of stew.

1 cup	green lentils	250 mL
1 tbsp	vegetable oil	15 mL
1	onion, chopped	1
2	stalks celery, chopped	2
1	large sweet red pepper, chopped	1
1	clove garlic, minced	1
1-2/3 cups	vegetable stock	400 mL
	Salt and pepper	
1-1/2 cups	water	375 mL
1 cup	couscous	250 mL
1 tsp	dried basil	5 mL
1/4 cup	chopped fresh parsley or basil	50 mL
1/4 cup	freshly grated Parmesan cheese	50 mL
1	tomato, chopped	1

● Rinse and sort lentils, discarding any discolored ones.

● In saucepan, heat oil over medium-high heat; cook onion, celery, red pepper and garlic, stirring often, for 5 minutes.

● Stir in lentils and stock; bring to boil. Reduce heat, cover and simmer, stirring occasionally, for 30 minutes or until lentils are tender. Season with salt and pepper to taste.

● Meanwhile, in saucepan, bring water to boil; stir in couscous and basil. Cover and remove from heat; let stand for 5 minutes. Fluff with fork. Stir in half of the parsley; season with salt and pepper to taste.

● Spoon couscous onto plates; top with ragout. Sprinkle with Parmesan, tomato and remaining parsley. Makes 4 servings.

Curried Squash Stew

The deep, rich flavor of this spicy vegetarian stew will please vegetarians and non-vegetarians alike. Add rice, warmed pita bread, and a cucumber sliced and dressed with yogurt and mint.

1/4 cup	vegetable oil	50 mL
2	onions, chopped	2
2	cloves garlic, minced	2
1 tbsp	curry powder	15 mL
2 tsp	ground cumin	10 mL
1 tsp	each chili powder, paprika and ground ginger	5 mL
1/2 tsp	salt	2 mL
3 lb	butternut squash	1.5 kg
2 cups	vegetable stock or water	500 mL
1	can (19 oz/540 mL) chick-peas, drained and rinsed	1
1/4 cup	currants	50 mL
1 tbsp	lemon juice	15 mL
1/4 cup	slivered almonds	50 mL

● In large Dutch oven, heat oil over medium heat; cook onions and garlic, stirring occasionally, for 4 minutes or until softened. Stir in curry powder, cumin, chili powder, paprika, ginger and salt; cook, stirring, for 2 minutes.

● Meanwhile, halve, seed and peel squash; cut into bite-size cubes. Add to pan along with stock, chick-peas and currants; bring to boil. Reduce heat, cover and simmer for 10 to 15 minutes or until squash is tender. Stir in lemon juice.

● Meanwhile, spread almonds on baking sheet; bake in 350°F (180°C) oven for 8 to 10 minutes or until golden. Sprinkle over stew. Makes 4 servings.

Chick-Pea and Tomato Stew with Basil

1 tbsp	olive oil	15 mL
1	onion, chopped	1
2	large cloves garlic, minced	2
3	large tomatoes, chopped	3
1/4 cup	chopped fresh basil (or 1/2 tsp/2 mL dried)	50 mL
1/2 tsp	paprika	2 mL
1/2 tsp	dried oregano	2 mL
2	potatoes, peeled and diced	2
1 cup	water or vegetable stock	250 mL
1	can (19 oz/540 mL) chick-peas, drained and rinsed	1
	Salt and pepper	
	Chopped fresh parsley	

● In large heavy saucepan, heat oil over medium heat; cook onion, stirring occasionally, for 3 to 5 minutes or until softened.

● Add garlic, 2 of the tomatoes, basil (if using dried), paprika and oregano; bring to boil. Reduce heat and simmer, stirring often, for 5 minutes or until slightly thickened.

● Add potatoes and water. Cover and bring to boil; cook, stirring occasionally, for 5 minutes. Add chick-peas; reduce heat and simmer for 3 to 5 minutes or until potatoes are tender.

● Add remaining tomato, basil (if using fresh), and salt and pepper to taste; heat for 1 minute. Garnish with parsley. Makes 3 servings.

Vegetarians don't have to resort to exotic and pricey ingredients from health food stores to make delicious, pleasing meals. This quick and inexpensive stew is just one example of how to prepare nutritious meatless meals with pizzazz.

Vegetarian Chili

1 cup	unsalted skinned peanuts (not dry-roasted), chopped	250 mL
2 tbsp	vegetable oil	25 mL
2 tsp	cumin seeds	10 mL
2	large onions, chopped	2
2 tbsp	ground coriander	25 mL
1 tsp	chili powder	5 mL
1 tsp	granulated sugar	5 mL
1/2 tsp	salt	2 mL
2	cans (each 28 oz/796 mL) tomatoes, chopped	2
2	cans (each 19 oz/540 mL) kidney beans	2
1/4 cup	chopped fresh parsley	50 mL

● In food processor and using on/off motion, grind peanuts finely; set aside.

● In large saucepan, heat oil over medium heat; cook cumin seeds, stirring often, for about 5 minutes or until beginning to crackle. Add peanuts; cook, stirring, for 3 minutes. Add onions, coriander, chili powder, sugar and salt; cook, stirring, for 3 minutes.

● Stir in tomatoes with juices; bring to boil. Reduce heat and simmer for about 10 minutes or until slightly thickened.

● Drain 1 of the cans of kidney beans. Add all beans and remaining liquid to pan; simmer for 5 minutes or until heated through. Garnish with parsley. Makes 6 servings.

Serve this mild and fragrant chili with homemade baked nacho chips (see below). Cooking the cumin seeds deepens and sweetens the spiciness they add to chili.

MAKE-YOUR-OWN NACHO CHIPS
Lighter nacho chips that are amazingly tasty and crunchy are a snap to make at home. Just cut round wheat tortillas into wedges; spread in a single layer on ungreased baking sheet and bake in 350°F (180°C) oven for about 6 minutes or until golden brown and crisp.

Satisfying Soups

In an era of bouillon cubes, cans of condensed and one-minute powders, cartons and pouches, here's soup the way it was meant to be — hearty, slow-simmered and full of homemade fresh flavor. Easy, too!

A Real Bargain of a Cabbage Soup ▶

This economical vegetarian soup was first served up at the Second Harvest, a Toronto food recovery program. Simmer a potful and rediscover the glories of real vegetables in real soup.

1/2 cup	white pea beans	125 mL
1/4 cup	vegetable oil	50 mL
1 cup	chopped onions	250 mL
1 tsp	dried basil	5 mL
1/2 tsp	dried oregano	2 mL
4 cups	shredded cabbage	1 L
1-1/2 cups	diced peeled potatoes	375 mL
1 cup	chopped celery	250 mL
3/4 cup	pearl or pot barley	175 mL
1	can (5-1/2 oz/156 mL) tomato paste	1
1/4 cup	shredded Cheddar cheese	50 mL
2 tbsp	chopped fresh parsley	25 mL
	Salt and pepper	

● Sort and rinse beans, discarding any blemished ones. In large saucepan or Dutch oven, cover beans with 3 times their volume of water; let stand overnight. (Alternatively, bring to boil and boil for 2 minutes. Cover and let stand for 1 hour.) Drain.

● In same pot, heat oil over medium-high heat; cook onions, stirring occasionally, for 3 to 5 minutes or until softened. Add 9 cups (2.25 L) water, beans, basil and oregano; bring to boil. Cover and reduce heat to medium-low; simmer, stirring occasionally, for 1 hour.

● Add cabbage, potatoes, celery and barley; blend in tomato paste. Cover and simmer for 35 to 40 minutes or until barley is cooked and beans and potatoes are tender. Stir in Cheddar and parsley. Season with salt and pepper to taste. Makes 8 servings.

THERE'S MORE TO SOUP THAN A PACK OF CRACKERS

● If crackers are the only thing you've ever served with a bowl of soup, why not try some of the delicious new breads and rolls now available in bakeries and markets across the country — crusty whole wheat rolls; pita and flat breads; multigrain breads with flax seed, sunflower seeds and yogurt, or loaves with olive oil and assorted herbs; Black Russian and caraway rye breads; Portuguese pada buns and dense cornbread; and trendy sourdough, pesto, olive or walnut and raisin breads. All are perfect for mopping up every last bit of soup, and turn a simple bowlful into a quick and nourishing meal.

● Ever-popular garlic bread is also a frequent partner for soup suppers — but most garlic breads are drenched in butter or oil. For a lighter version, slice sourdough or other firm Mediterranean bread thickly, rub slices on both sides with crushed garlic, brush very lightly with olive oil and toast under the broiler or in the toaster oven.

Smoky Bean Soup ▲

A few reliables in the pantry, crisper and refrigerator make it convenient to simmer up a hearty supper soup. Leftovers reheat deliciously for lunch the next day.

1 cup	white pea beans	250 mL
1	large onion, minced	1
2	stalks celery, chopped	2
2	large carrots, diced	2
3 cups	beef stock	750 mL
3 cups	water	750 mL
1/4 cup	minced fresh parsley (or 2 tbsp/25 mL dried)	50 mL
1/2 tsp	pepper	2 mL
8 oz	smoked sausage, chopped	250 g
	Salt	

● Sort and rinse beans, discarding any blemished ones. In large saucepan or Dutch oven, cover beans with 3 times their volume of water; let stand overnight. (Alternatively, bring to boil; boil for 2 minutes. Cover and let stand for 1 hour.) Drain.

● In same pot, combine beans, onion, celery, carrots, beef stock, water, parsley, pepper and sausage; bring to boil. Reduce heat, cover and simmer for 1 to 1-1/4 hours or until beans are tender. Skim off any fat. Season with salt to taste. Makes 4 to 6 servings.

Bean Bag Vegetable Soup

1-1/2 cups	Bean Bag Soup Mix (recipe follows)	375 mL
1	can (28 oz/796 mL) tomatoes	1
1	large onion, chopped	1
1	large carrot, chopped	1
8 oz	sliced smoked sausage or cubed ham	250 g
2 tsp	chili powder	10 mL
Pinch	ground cloves	Pinch
2 tbsp	dry sherry (optional)	25 mL
1 tbsp	lemon juice	15 mL
	Salt and pepper	

● Rinse Bean Bag Soup Mix. In large saucepan or Dutch oven, cover bean mix with 3 times its volume of water; let stand overnight. (Alternatively, bring to boil and boil for 2 minutes. Cover and let stand for 1 hour.) Drain.

● In same pot, combine bean mix with 6 cups (1.5 L) water; bring to boil. Reduce heat, cover and simmer for about 1-1/2 hours or until tender.

● Add tomatoes, breaking up with fork; add onion, carrot, sausage, chili powder and cloves; bring to boil. Reduce heat and simmer for 30 minutes. Skim off any fat. Stir in sherry (if using) and lemon juice; season with salt and pepper to taste. Makes 8 servings.

BEAN BAG SOUP MIX
● Discarding any blemished beans, peas or lentils, mix together 1 cup (250 mL) each split red lentils and pearl barley and 1-1/4 cups (300 mL) each pinto beans, kidney beans, small lima beans, great Northern beans, yellow split peas, green split peas, whole green peas and whole green lentils. Makes 12 cups (3 L).

Although you can buy bean blends in most bulk food stores, it's much more satisfying to make your own. Why not bag some up as gifts for family and friends — as they do every year at the Christmas bazaar at Vancouver's historic Hycroft house. Be sure to attach the recipe for the vegetable soup.

Quick Chunky Minestrone Nice soup Aug 9/95

4	slices bacon, diced	4
2	stalks celery, sliced	2
1	onion, chopped	1
1	carrot, thinly sliced	1
1	clove garlic, minced	1
1	can (19 oz/540 mL) tomatoes	1
4 cups	chicken stock	1 L
4 oz	green beans, sliced	125 g
1/4 tsp	each crumbled dried sage and thyme	1 mL
1	can (19 oz/540 mL) chick-peas, drained and rinsed	1
1/4 cup	macaroni	50 mL
	Salt and pepper	
1/4 cup	freshly grated Parmesan cheese	50 mL

● In large saucepan, cook bacon over medium heat until crisp; remove with slotted spoon and set aside.

● Pour off all but 1 tbsp (15 mL) drippings from pan. Add celery, onion, carrot and garlic; cook, stirring occasionally, for 5 minutes. Add tomatoes, breaking up with back of spoon. Add chicken stock, beans, sage and thyme; bring to boil. Reduce heat, cover and simmer for 5 minutes.

● Add chick-peas and macaroni; cook for 8 to 10 minutes or until macaroni is tender but firm. Return bacon to pan. Season with salt and pepper to taste. *(Minestrone can be cooled in refrigerator and stored in airtight container for up to 2 days or frozen for up to 3 months.)* Top each serving with Parmesan. Makes 4 servings.

Canned chick-peas save on time needed to make this Italian classic.

Tomato Clam Chowder ▼

The ingredient list may look a bit long, but this pleasing meal-in-a-bowl is really fast and effortless to put together.

1 tbsp	vegetable oil	15 mL
2	onions, chopped	2
2	stalks celery, chopped	2
2 tsp	dried thyme	10 mL
1	bay leaf	1
2	cans (each 5 oz/142 g) baby clams	2
1	can (28 oz/796 mL) tomatoes	1
1	bottle (237 mL) clam juice	1
1	potato, peeled and diced	1
1	zucchini, diced	1
2	strips orange rind	2
2 tbsp	tomato paste	25 mL
2 tbsp	chopped fresh parsley	25 mL
3/4 tsp	salt	4 mL
1/4 tsp	pepper	1 mL
Dash	hot pepper sauce	Dash

● In Dutch oven, heat oil over medium heat; cook onions, celery, thyme and bay leaf, stirring occasionally, for about 5 minutes or until softened.

● Drain clams, adding juice to pan; rinse clams and set aside. Add tomatoes to pan, breaking up with back of spoon.

● Stir in bottled clam juice, potato, zucchini, orange rind and tomato paste; bring to boil. Reduce heat, cover and simmer for 10 minutes. Uncover and simmer for 10 minutes longer or until slightly thickened and potatoes are tender.

● Stir in clams, parsley, salt, pepper and hot pepper sauce; heat through. Discard bay leaf and orange rind. Makes 4 servings.

TRENDY FOCACCIA

Focaccia, an Italian herbed flat bread, is a delicious companion to any soup meal. To make an easy version at home, brush store-bought baked pizza crust with olive oil, then sprinkle with crumbled rosemary and a bit of Parmesan, if desired. Heat briefly in the oven or toaster oven until crisp.

Mediterranean Fish Soup with Croutes

12 oz	mussels	375 g
1 tbsp	olive oil	15 mL
2	cloves garlic, minced	2
1	onion, chopped	1
1	leek (white part), sliced	1
1 tbsp	tomato paste	15 mL
2	tomatoes, peeled, seeded and chopped	2
4 cups	fish stock or chicken stock	1 L
1/2 cup	dry white wine	125 mL
1/2 tsp	fennel seeds	2 mL
1/2 tsp	grated orange rind	2 mL
1/4 tsp	saffron threads	1 mL
Pinch	crushed dried thyme	Pinch
1	bay leaf	1
1 lb	monkfish	500 g
1 lb	cod or haddock	500 g
	Salt and pepper	
	Croutes (recipe follows)	
	Roasted Pepper Spread (recipe follows)	
1/4 cup	chopped fresh parsley	50 mL
	Strips orange rind (optional)	

● Scrub mussels under running water and remove any beards; discard any that do not close when tapped. Set aside.

● In large saucepan, heat oil over medium heat; cook garlic, onion and leek, stirring occasionally, for 5 minutes or until softened.

● Stir in tomato paste. Add tomatoes, fish stock, wine, fennel seeds, grated orange rind, saffron, thyme and bay leaf; cook over high heat, stirring occasionally, for 5 minutes or until boiling and thickened slightly.

● Meanwhile, cut monkfish and cod into 2-inch (5 cm) chunks; add to soup. Reduce heat to medium; cook for 5 minutes. Add mussels; cook for 4 minutes or until fish is opaque and mussels open. Discard any mussels that do not open. Discard bay leaf. Season soup with salt and pepper to taste.

● Spread each Croute with some Roasted Pepper Spread; place 1 on bottom of each warmed soup bowl. Ladle soup into bowls; sprinkle with parsley. Garnish with orange rind strips (if using). Pass remaining Roasted Pepper Spread separately to stir into soup, if desired. Makes 6 servings.

CROUTES

6	thick slices French stick (baguette)	6

● Arrange bread on baking sheet; bake in 350°F (180°C) oven for 15 minutes or until lightly browned. Makes 6 croutes.

ROASTED PEPPER SPREAD

1	sweet red pepper	1
3	cloves garlic, minced	3
2 tbsp	olive oil	25 mL
Dash	hot pepper sauce	Dash
2 tbsp	dry bread crumbs	25 mL
	Salt	

● Broil red pepper, turning several times, for about 20 minutes or until blistered and charred. Let cool; peel and seed.

● In food processor or blender, purée roasted red pepper and garlic until smooth. Blend in oil and hot pepper sauce. Stir in bread crumbs until blended. Season with salt to taste. Makes 1/2 cup (125 mL).

I*f you like croutons, you'll love these big-version croutes — whole slices of bread toasted until crusty, then spread with a garlicky roasted pepper mixture, laid in a soup bowl and topped with ladlefuls of soup swimming with seafood and redolent of tomatoes, thyme and fennel.*

Potato Broccoli Chowder

When broccoli snobs have eaten up all the florets, use up the stalks in this quick thick soup. Just be sure to peel off their fibrous outer layer.

4 cups	diced peeled potatoes	1 L
2-1/2 cups	chicken stock	625 mL
1 cup	diced ham	250 mL
2	onions, chopped	2
1	clove garlic, minced	1
1/2 tsp	dried marjoram	2 mL
2-1/2 cups	diced broccoli	625 mL
2 cups	milk	500 mL
Dash	hot pepper sauce	Dash
	Salt and pepper	
3/4 cup	shredded Cheddar cheese	175 mL

● In large saucepan, combine potatoes, chicken stock, ham, onions, garlic and marjoram; bring to boil. Reduce heat, cover and simmer for about 15 minutes or until potatoes are nearly tender.

● Add broccoli and return to simmer; cook for 5 to 7 minutes or until tender-crisp. Add milk, hot pepper sauce, and salt and pepper to taste; heat through. Sprinkle each serving with Cheddar. Makes 6 servings.

TIP: To make this soup vegetarian, omit ham and simmer potatoes in vegetable stock (save your own vegetable cooking liquid or use powdered stock).

Corn and Cheddar Chowder

Chock-full of summer's best vegetables, this easy chowder for two makes a great meal with a spinach salad.

2 tsp	butter	10 mL
1	onion, chopped	1
1	clove garlic, minced	1
1	each carrot and stalk celery, diced	1
1-1/2 cups	diced new potatoes (8 oz/250 g)	375 mL
1 tbsp	all-purpose flour	15 mL
1-1/2 tsp	chopped fresh thyme (or 1/2 tsp/2 mL dried)	7 mL
1/4 tsp	each salt and pepper	1 mL
1	bay leaf	1
Pinch	hot pepper flakes	Pinch
1 cup	vegetable or chicken stock	250 mL
1-1/4 cups	milk	300 mL
1 cup	corn kernels	250 mL
1 cup	shredded old Cheddar cheese	250 mL
1/4 cup	diced sweet red pepper	50 mL

● In saucepan, melt butter over medium heat; cook onion, garlic, carrot, celery and potatoes, stirring often, for 3 minutes. Sprinkle with flour, thyme, salt, pepper, bay leaf and hot pepper flakes; cook, stirring, for 30 seconds.

● Gradually whisk in stock; bring to boil. Reduce heat, cover and simmer for about 10 minutes or until potatoes are just tender.

● Stir in milk and corn; cover and cook over low heat for about 8 minutes or until corn is tender. *(Chowder can be prepared to this point, cooled in refrigerator and stored in airtight container for up to 1 day; reheat over low heat.)*

● Add Cheddar; cook, stirring often, just until melted. Discard bay leaf. Garnish with red pepper. Makes 2 servings.

Cape Breton Fish Chowder ▲

1 lb	mussels	500 g
1/4 cup	butter	50 mL
3	potatoes, diced	3
2	stalks celery, diced	2
1	carrot, diced	1
1	onion, diced	1
1	clove garlic, minced	1
1/4 cup	all-purpose flour	50 mL
6 cups	chicken stock	1.5 L
8 oz	boneless skinless salmon, cubed	250 g
4 oz	scallops, sliced	125 g
1/4 cup	whipping cream	50 mL
4 tsp	each chopped fresh dill and basil	20 mL
1/4 tsp	pepper	1 mL

● Scrub mussels under running water and remove any beards; discard any that do not close when tapped. Set aside.

● In large heavy saucepan, melt butter over medium-high heat; cook potatoes, celery, carrot, onion and garlic, stirring often, for 8 minutes or until softened.

● Stir in flour. Gradually whisk in 5 cups (1.25 L) of the stock; bring to boil. Reduce heat, cover and simmer for about 10 minutes or until vegetables are tender.

● Meanwhile, in separate saucepan, bring remaining stock to boil. Reduce heat to simmer and poach salmon for 1 minute; remove with slotted spoon and set aside. Poach scallops for 1 minute; with slotted spoon, add to salmon. Add mussels to pan; cover and poach for 3 minutes or until mussels open. With slotted spoon, add mussels to salmon, discarding any mussels that do not open.

● Strain poaching liquid into vegetable mixture. Add cream, dill, basil and pepper; heat through. Add reserved seafood; heat through until steaming. Makes 6 servings.

A *Maritime classic, this fine chowder graces the tables at the Markland, a resort at the tip of Cape Breton, Nova Scotia. Note that the seafood is simmered separately to make sure it doesn't overcook.*

Big-Batch Portuguese Pumpkin Soup

The sweetness of cinnamon pairs up with smoky bacon and aromatic cumin to make an utterly delicious soup. Crusty Portuguese bread will mop your bowl clean.

4 oz	dried chorizo sausage	125 g
4 oz	lean bacon or pork hock	125 g
1	large onion, halved	1
1	clove garlic	1
10 cups	chicken stock or water	2.5 L
4	sweet potatoes (about 2 lb/1 kg)	4
2	potatoes	2
1	small pumpkin or squash (about 4 lb/2 kg)	1
1	stick (4-inch/10 cm) cinnamon	1
2 tsp	ground cumin	10 mL
1 tsp	whole allspice	5 mL
	Salt	

● In large saucepan or Dutch oven, combine chorizo, bacon, onion, garlic and chicken stock; cover and bring to boil. Reduce heat and simmer for 20 minutes, skimming off all foam.

● Meanwhile, peel and quarter sweet and white potatoes. Cut pumpkin in half; scoop out seeds and discard. Using sharp knife, peel pumpkin; cut pulp into large cubes.

● Add sweet and white potatoes, pumpkin, cinnamon, cumin and allspice to pan; bring to boil. Reduce heat, cover and simmer for 20 to 25 minutes or until meat and vegetables are tender.

● Discard cinnamon and allspice. Remove chorizo and bacon; chop into bite-size pieces and set aside.

● Using slotted spoon, transfer vegetables to food processor or blender; purée, in batches if necessary, until smooth. Return purée and meat to saucepan and heat through; season with salt to taste. Makes 12 servings.

TIP: Chorizo is the Spanish spelling for the spicy paprika garlic sausage called chourice in Portuguese.

Autumn Harvest Soup

A tureen of soup sounds a note of welcome for weekend get-togethers. Add to the flavor and fun by setting out bowls of toppings to spoon over each serving — air-popped popcorn, croutons, coarsely crushed nacho chips, chopped green onion or chives, shredded carrots, sour cream, pesto or slivered red pepper.

2 tbsp	butter	25 mL
1 tbsp	vegetable oil	15 mL
2	leeks, sliced	2
1	onion, chopped	1
6 cups	cubed peeled squash (about 2 lb/500 g)	1.5 L
1	potato, peeled and diced	1
4 cups	chicken stock	1 L
1/2 tsp	salt	2 mL
1/4 tsp	white pepper	1 mL
Pinch	cayenne pepper	Pinch
1 cup	light cream or milk	250 mL

● In large saucepan, melt butter with oil over medium-low heat; cook leeks and onion, covered and stirring often, for 10 minutes or until softened but not browned.

● Add squash, potato, chicken stock, salt, white pepper and cayenne; bring to boil. Cover and reduce heat to medium-low; simmer for 20 minutes or until vegetables are tender.

● In batches, transfer to food processor or blender and purée. *(Soup can be prepared to this point, cooled in refrigerator and frozen in airtight containers for up to 2 weeks; thaw before continuing.)* Return soup to saucepan. Add cream; heat through but do not boil. Makes 6 to 8 servings.

Lentil Barley Potage

2 cups	green lentils	500 mL
2 tsp	vegetable oil	10 mL
1	onion, chopped	1
2	cloves garlic, minced	2
8 oz	kielbasa or other smoked sausage, chopped	250 g
5 cups	chicken stock	1.25 L
5 cups	water	1.25 L
1/2 cup	pearl or pot barley	125 mL
1	bay leaf	1
1 tsp	dried marjoram	5 mL
1/2 tsp	dried thyme	2 mL
1 cup	each sliced carrot and celery	250 mL
1/4 cup	chopped fresh parsley	50 mL
	Salt and pepper	

● Sort and rinse lentils, discarding any blemished ones; set aside.

● In large saucepan or Dutch oven, heat oil over medium heat; cook onion and garlic, stirring occasionally, for 3 minutes or until softened. Add sausage; cook, stirring occasionally, for 5 minutes.

● Add chicken stock, water, lentils, barley, bay leaf, marjoram and thyme; bring to boil. Reduce heat to medium-low; cover and simmer for 20 minutes.

● Add carrot and celery; simmer for about 25 minutes or until lentils and barley are tender. Discard bay leaf. *(Soup can be prepared to this point, cooled in refrigerator and frozen in airtight container for up to 2 weeks; reheat gently.)* Stir in parsley; season with salt and pepper to taste. Makes 6 to 8 servings.

Lest we get carried away with how delicious lentils are, don't forget they're also an excellent source of fiber and a good source of iron and vitamins A and B. Serve with crisper crudités, a low-fat dip and pumpernickel bread.

Hamburger Goulash Soup

8 oz	lean ground beef	250 g
1	onion, chopped	1
1-1/2 cups	sliced mushrooms (about 4 oz/125 g)	375 mL
Half	sweet green pepper, chopped	Half
1 tbsp	paprika	15 mL
2 tsp	caraway seeds, crushed	10 mL
1 tsp	each dried basil and marjoram	5 mL
1/4 tsp	each salt and pepper	1 mL
3-1/2 cups	beef stock	875 mL
1	can (10 oz/284 mL) stewed tomatoes	1
2 cups	diced peeled potatoes	500 mL
1 cup	chopped carrots	250 mL
1/2 cup	chopped zucchini	125 mL
1/2 cup	corn kernels	125 mL

● In large saucepan or Dutch oven, cook beef over medium-high heat, breaking up with back of spoon, for 5 minutes or until no longer pink; drain off fat. Add onion, mushrooms and green pepper; cook, stirring occasionally, for 6 to 8 minutes or until onion is softened.

● Reduce heat to low; stir in paprika, caraway seeds, basil, marjoram, salt and pepper. Cover and cook, stirring occasionally, for 10 minutes.

● Add beef stock, tomatoes, potatoes and carrots; bring to boil. Reduce heat to medium-low; cover and simmer for 15 minutes.

● Stir in zucchini and corn; cover and cook for 5 to 10 minutes or until vegetables are tender. Makes 4 to 6 servings.

With no meat to cut into chunks and no added fat for browning, lean ground beef makes this vegetable-rich goulash soup a quick and convenient bowlful of supper. Round out the menu with whole wheat rolls and fruit.

Whole-Meal Salads

We've tossed together a satisfying selection of leafy greens,
meat and seafood hot off the skillet or grill, easy pasta, crunchy-
fresh vegetables and zingy vinaigrettes.

Warm Beef Stir-Fry Salad ▶

*Stir-fried beef, yellow
peppers and mushrooms,
all still warm from the wok,
dress up a plate of colorful
summer lettuces.*

1	head butter lettuce	1
1	head radicchio or red lettuce	1
1	small head romaine lettuce	1
12 oz	sirloin steak	375 g
1	large sweet yellow or green pepper	1
1 tbsp	vegetable oil	15 mL
3 cups	sliced mushrooms (8 oz/250 g)	750 mL
1/4 tsp	salt	1 mL
1 cup	large cherry tomatoes, quartered	250 mL
2 tbsp	chopped fresh thyme (or 1-1/2 tsp/7 mL dried)	25 mL
	DRESSING	
3 tbsp	balsamic vinegar or red wine vinegar	50 mL
1 tsp	Dijon mustard	5 mL
1	clove garlic, minced	1
1/2 tsp	each salt and pepper	2 mL
1/3 cup	extra virgin olive oil	75 mL

● Separate leaves of butter, radicchio and romaine lettuces; tear into bite-size pieces and toss together in large salad bowl.

● DRESSING: In small bowl, combine vinegar, mustard, garlic, salt and pepper; whisk in oil. Set aside.

● Slice steak on the diagonal into thin slices. Cut yellow pepper into 1/2-inch (1 cm) wide strips.

● Heat wok or large skillet over high heat; add 2 tsp (10 mL) of the oil, swirling to coat pan. Stir-fry beef, in batches, for about 2 minutes or just until no longer pink. Remove and keep warm.

● Add remaining oil to wok; stir-fry yellow pepper, mushrooms and salt for 2 minutes or just until mushrooms begin to release liquid. Add to salad bowl along with beef, tomatoes and thyme; toss with dressing. Serve immediately. Makes 4 servings.

A GUIDE TO GREENS

● **Belgian Endive**: Small, white, oval-shaped head with pale yellow-tipped leaves. Grown in darkness to prevent it from turning green; exposure to light makes it bitter.

● **Butter (Boston, Bibb)**: Small, round, loosely formed head of pale green leaves. It has a soft, buttery texture and a slightly sweet flavor.

● **Curly Endive:** Bunchy head with narrow, lacy, pale green, frilly-tipped outer leaves. It has a slightly bitter taste.

● **Leaf**: Any of several varieties that branch from a single stalk to form a ruffled loose bunch rather than a tightly coiled head. Generally full-flavored, two decorative varieties are oak and red leaf.

● **Radicchio:** Radicchio has a slightly bitter flavor. The two most common varieties are: di Verona, a round, deep burgundy head of shiny, smooth leaves with white central ribs; and di Treviso, with pink to deep red spear-shaped leaves in a head that resembles a narrow tulip.

● **Romaine:** Long loaf-shaped head with dark green outer leaves and pale yellow inner ones. Its leaves are crisp and have a mildly bitter flavor.

BLT Salad

Bacon, lettuce and tomatoes — grand in a sandwich, dynamite in a salad for supper or lunch.

8	slices bacon	8
2 tbsp	olive oil	25 mL
1	clove garlic, minced	1
6	slices bread	6
6 cups	shredded romaine lettuce	1.5 L
3	green onions, sliced	3
4	large tomatoes, cubed	4
	Salt and pepper	
	DRESSING	
1/2 cup	buttermilk	125 mL
1/3 cup	light mayonnaise	75 mL
1/2 tsp	Dijon mustard	2 mL
1	clove garlic, minced	1

● In skillet, cook bacon over high heat until crisp; drain on paper towels. Crumble and set aside.

● Meanwhile, combine oil with garlic; brush over bread. Cut into cubes; bake on baking sheet in 350°F (180°C) oven for 10 minutes or until golden. Let cool.

● In salad bowl, combine lettuce, onions, tomatoes, bacon and bread cubes.

● DRESSING: Whisk together buttermilk, mayonnaise, mustard and garlic; toss with salad. Season with salt and pepper to taste. Makes 4 servings.

Red Bean and Lamb Salad

Lamb with red kidney beans, cumin and fresh coriander gives a nineties twist to a main-course salad classic. Cold roast or grilled beef or pork can replace the lamb. Serve with crusty bread, tortillas or pitas.

Half	red onion, chopped	Half
2 cups	diced cooked lamb	500 mL
4	tomatoes, diced	4
1	sweet green pepper, diced	1
2/3 cup	sliced celery	150 mL
1	can (19 oz/540 mL) red kidney beans, drained and rinsed	1
1/4 cup	red wine vinegar	50 mL
2 tbsp	vegetable oil	25 mL
1 tsp	ground cumin	5 mL
1/2 tsp	salt	2 mL
1/4 tsp	hot pepper sauce	1 mL
2 tbsp	chopped fresh coriander or parsley	25 mL
3/4 cup	light sour cream	175 mL

● Soak onion in cold water for 15 minutes; drain and pat dry.

● In large bowl, combine lamb, tomatoes, green pepper, celery, kidney beans and onion.

● Whisk together vinegar, oil, cumin, salt and hot pepper sauce; drizzle over salad and toss lightly.

● Stir coriander into sour cream; serve as sauce with salad. Makes 4 servings.

CLEAN GREENS

1 Cut out core or stem from lettuce; separate leaves.

2 In cold water, gently swish leaves to clean well. (For tightly curled heads, such as iceberg and Belgian endive, just remove outer leaves and wash head.)

3 Place leaves in colander or towel, shaking off excess water. Discard any wilted leaves; tear off any discolored parts.

4 Loosely fill salad spinner half-full with greens; spin, pouring off water occasionally. Blot leaves gently with towel to remove any remaining moisture.

5 Layer greens loosely between dry towels; roll up and place in plastic bag. Store in refrigerator for up to 5 days.

Spaghetti Tuna Salad ▼

Nothing could be easier than this spaghetti salad with sunny olive, tomato and basil highlights.

12 oz	spaghetti	375 g
1/4 cup	extra virgin olive oil	50 mL
1-1/2 tsp	salt	7 mL
1/2 tsp	pepper	2 mL
1/4 tsp	hot pepper flakes (optional)	1 mL
2	cloves garlic, minced	2
4	tomatoes, diced	4
2	cans (each 6-1/2 oz/184 g) tuna, drained and flaked	2
1/3 cup	sliced pitted black olives	75 mL
1/4 cup	each chopped fresh parsley and basil	50 mL
2	green onions, chopped	2

● In large pot of boiling salted water, cook spaghetti for 8 to 10 minutes or until tender but firm; drain well.

● Meanwhile, in large bowl, combine oil, salt, pepper, hot pepper flakes (if using) and garlic. Stir in tomatoes, tuna, olives, parsley, basil and onions. Add spaghetti; toss to combine. Makes 4 servings.

Mediterranean Couscous Salad

1-3/4 cups	water	425 mL
1/2 tsp	salt	2 mL
1-1/4 cups	couscous	300 mL
1/3 cup	chopped green onions	75 mL
2	tomatoes, diced	2
1 cup	diced feta cheese (4 oz/125 g)	250 mL
1/2 cup	black olives, pitted and quartered	125 mL
2 tbsp	each chopped fresh mint and oregano	25 mL
1/3 cup	extra virgin olive oil	75 mL
1/4 cup	lemon juice	50 mL
	Pepper	

● In saucepan, bring water and salt to boil; stir in couscous. Cover and remove from heat; let stand for 4 minutes. Fluff with fork.

● In large bowl, combine couscous, green onions, tomatoes, feta cheese, olives, mint and oregano.

● Whisk together oil and lemon juice; pour over salad and toss to combine. Season with pepper to taste. Makes 4 servings.

Feta, mint and oregano bring the sunny flavors of Greece to a light-meal couscous salad.

Chicken and Pear Salad

*W*hen it's a substantial salad you're seeking, look no further. This is a perfect easy-to-assemble one-dish meal of crispy greens, shredded chicken (or turkey, if you have holiday leftovers), pears, toasted walnuts and crumbled blue cheese in a memorable vinaigrette dressing.

8 cups	torn salad greens (endive, romaine, escarole)	2 L
2 cups	shredded cooked chicken (see above)	500 mL
Half	red onion, slivered	Half
2	firm ripe pears	2
1-1/2 oz	blue cheese, crumbled	40 g
1/3 cup	walnut pieces or halves, toasted (see TIP below)	75 mL
	Herbed Croutons (recipe follows)	

HONEY TARRAGON VINAIGRETTE		
3 tbsp	white wine vinegar	50 mL
1	clove garlic, minced	1
2 tbsp	minced shallot or green onions	25 mL
2 tbsp	liquid honey	25 mL
1 tbsp	Dijon mustard	15 mL
1-1/2 tsp	dried tarragon	7 mL
1/2 tsp	salt	2 mL
1/3 cup	walnut or extra virgin olive oil	75 mL

● HONEY TARRAGON VINAIGRETTE: In bowl, whisk together vinegar, garlic, shallot, honey, mustard, tarragon and salt; gradually whisk in oil.

● In salad bowl, combine salad greens, chicken and onion. Core and quarter pears; slice into 1/4-inch (5 mm) thick wedges and add to bowl. Toss with vinaigrette. Sprinkle with cheese, walnuts and Herbed Croutons; toss again. Makes 6 servings.

HERBED CROUTONS		
1 cup	cubed day-old crusty bread	250 mL
2 tbsp	olive oil	25 mL
1/2 tsp	each dried thyme and tarragon	2 mL
	Salt	

● In bowl, toss together bread, oil, thyme and tarragon; bake on baking sheet in 350°F (180°C) oven for 10 minutes or until golden. Season with salt to taste. Let cool. Makes 1 cup (250 mL).

TIP: To toast walnuts, spread on baking sheet and bake in 350°F (180°C) oven for 6 to 10 minutes or until fragrant.

Grilled Chicken Salad ▼

1/4 cup	extra virgin olive oil	50 mL
1/4 cup	chicken stock	50 mL
3 tbsp	lemon juice	45 mL
2 tbsp	each chopped fresh basil and oregano (or 1 tsp/5 mL dried)	25 mL
2 tsp	minced jalapeño pepper	10 mL
1 tsp	Dijon mustard	5 mL
1/4 tsp	each salt and pepper	1 mL
1	red onion	1
4	boneless skinless chicken breasts	4
8 cups	torn salad greens	2 L
3/4 cup	crumbled feta cheese	175 mL

● In small saucepan, whisk together oil, chicken stock, lemon juice, half each of the basil and oregano (or all, if using dried), the jalapeño, mustard, salt and pepper; remove 2 tbsp (25 mL) and set aside. Place saucepan over low heat to warm vinaigrette.

● Cut onion into 1/2-inch (1 cm) thick rounds. Brush both sides of onion and chicken with reserved vinaigrette. Place on greased grill over medium heat; cook for 6 to 7 minutes per side or until chicken is no longer pink inside. Cut chicken into 1/2-inch (1 cm) thick slices. Separate onion into rings.

● In salad bowl, toss together chicken, onion, salad greens and warm vinaigrette until coated. Sprinkle with feta cheese and remaining fresh basil and oregano. Makes 4 servings.

Y*ou can still make this salad after grilling season. Either cook the chicken breasts in a ridged cast-iron grill pan, or pan-fry in the very tiniest amount of oil. Instead of grilling the thickly sliced onion, choose a smaller onion, slice it very thinly and add it to the salad, ungrilled, at the end.*

Caribbean Chicken Salad

This refreshing tropical main-course salad is ideal for those scorching summer days when it's too hot even to barbecue. For an authentic touch, look for Jamaican curry powder.

2-1/2 cups	cubed cooked chicken breast (see p. 76)	625 mL
1/2 cup	chopped celery	125 mL
1/2 cup	finely chopped green onions	125 mL
2	large mangoes, peeled and cut into chunks	2
1/2 cup	unsalted cashews or almonds, coarsely chopped	125 mL
	Salt and pepper	
4	leaves butter lettuce	4
	CURRY VINAIGRETTE	
1/4 cup	vegetable oil	50 mL
2 tbsp	lime juice	25 mL
1-1/2 tsp	curry powder	7 mL
1 tsp	grated gingerroot	5 mL
1	large clove garlic, minced	1
1/2 tsp	salt	2 mL
1/2 tsp	Dijon mustard	2 mL

● CURRY VINAIGRETTE: In small jar with tight-fitting lid, shake together oil, lime juice, curry powder, ginger, garlic, salt and mustard.

● In large bowl, gently toss together chicken, celery, green onions, mangoes, cashews and vinaigrette; season with salt and pepper to taste. Serve in lettuce leaf cups. Makes 4 servings.

Pasta Shrimp Salad for a Crowd

A refreshing lemon-dill buttermilk dressing pairs up perfectly with shrimp and cherry tomatoes in a pasta salad that goes light on the mayo.

4 cups	rotini or fusilli	1 L
2 cups	frozen peas	500 mL
2	each small green and yellow zucchini, cubed	2
2 tbsp	vegetable oil	25 mL
2	sweet red peppers, diced	2
1 cup	chopped green onions	250 mL
1 cup	diced celery	250 mL
1 lb	small cocktail shrimp, thawed	500 g
2 cups	cherry tomatoes, halved	500 mL
	Fresh dill sprigs	
	DRESSING	
1 cup	light mayonnaise	250 mL
1/2 cup	chopped fresh dill	125 mL
1/2 cup	buttermilk	125 mL
1/2 cup	light sour cream	125 mL
1 tbsp	grated lemon rind	15 mL
2 tbsp	lemon juice	25 mL
2 tbsp	Dijon mustard	25 mL
2	cloves garlic, minced	2
2 tsp	salt	10 mL
1 tsp	pepper	5 mL

● In large pot of boiling salted water, cook rotini for 6 minutes. Add peas and green and yellow zucchini; cook for 2 minutes or until rotini is tender but firm. Drain and refresh under cold water; drain again and transfer to large bowl.

● Add oil; toss to coat. Add red peppers, green onions and celery. *(Salad can be prepared to this point, covered and refrigerated for up to 1 day.)*

● DRESSING: In small bowl, whisk together mayonnaise, dill, buttermilk, sour cream, lemon rind and juice, mustard, garlic, salt and pepper.

● Pat shrimp dry; add to pasta mixture along with dressing and toss to coat. *(Salad can be covered and refrigerated for up to 4 hours.)* Garnish with cherry tomatoes and dill sprigs. Makes 16 servings.

Make-Ahead Penne Salad

2 cups	penne	500 mL
1/2 cup	snow peas	125 mL
1/3 cup	mayonnaise-style salad dressing	75 mL
2 tbsp	tomato juice	25 mL
1 tbsp	white wine vinegar	15 mL
1-1/2 tsp	Dijon mustard	7 mL
1/4 tsp	each salt and pepper	1 mL
1/4 cup	chopped fresh chives	50 mL
1/4 cup	chopped fresh parsley	50 mL
2 tbsp	chopped fresh dill	25 mL
1 cup	drained canned chick-peas	250 mL
1/2 cup	sliced celery	125 mL
1	each sweet red and green pepper, cut into strips	1

● In large pot of boiling salted water, cook penne for 8 to 10 minutes or until tender but firm. Drain and refresh under cold water; drain well.

● Meanwhile, trim snow peas; blanch in small pot of boiling water for 1 minute. Drain and refresh under cold water; drain again.

● In large bowl, whisk together salad dressing, tomato juice, vinegar, mustard, salt and pepper; mix in chives, parsley and dill. Add penne, snow peas, chick-peas, celery and red and green pepper; toss to coat well. *(Salad can be covered and refrigerated for up to 1 day.)* Makes 4 servings.

Pasta salads, like this one with chives and dill, are favorites to take to potluck meals and away for the weekend.

Couscous and Chick-Pea Salad

1 cup	couscous	250 mL
1/2 cup	raisins	125 mL
1 cup	drained canned chick-peas	250 mL
4 oz	sliced ham, julienned	125 g
1/4 cup	chopped fresh parsley	50 mL
3	green onions, sliced	3
1	tomato, diced	1
1	sweet red pepper, diced	1
1	small zucchini, diced	1
1/2 cup	extra virgin olive oil	125 mL
3 tbsp	lemon juice	45 mL
1	clove garlic, minced	1
3/4 tsp	salt	4 mL
1/2 tsp	ground cumin	2 mL
1/4 tsp	turmeric	1 mL
Dash	hot pepper sauce	Dash

● In saucepan, bring 1-1/4 cups (300 mL) water to boil; stir in couscous and raisins. Cover and remove from heat; let stand for 5 minutes. Fluff with fork.

● In large bowl, combine couscous mixture, chick-peas, ham, parsley, onions, tomato, red pepper and zucchini.

● Whisk together oil, lemon juice, garlic, salt, cumin, turmeric and hot pepper sauce; toss with salad until combined. Makes 4 servings.

TIP: When a recipe says to "julienne" an ingredient (usually peppers, carrots or ham), all it means is to cut into strips. Depending on time, the cook's inclination and the recipe, the strips can be as small as matchsticks or as generous as a thin stubby pencil.

Here's to easy cooking and summer in a bowl — ham, tomatoes, red pepper and zucchini on a bed of flavorful chick-peas and couscous. Look for couscous, a wheat product, in bulk food stores and some supermarkets.

Warm Potato Salad with Brie ▼

Choose waxy-textured potatoes for salads. Round new potatoes are the tastiest choice, especially in season. For extra texture and color, do not peel salad-bound potatoes.

6	new potatoes (1-1/2 lb/750 g)	6
1/3 cup	extra virgin olive oil	75 mL
2 tbsp	white wine vinegar	25 mL
1 tbsp	Dijon mustard	15 mL
1/2 cup	sliced red onion	125 mL
4 oz	Brie or Camembert cheese, cubed	125 g
	Salt and pepper	
4 cups	torn lettuce	1 L
6	radishes, sliced	6
	Chopped fresh parsley	

● Scrub potatoes; cut into 1/2-inch (1 cm) cubes. In saucepan of boiling salted water, cook potatoes for about 10 minutes or just until tender. Drain well and return to pot.

● Whisk together oil, vinegar and mustard; stir into potatoes. Sprinkle with onion and Brie. Warm over low heat for 1 to 2 minutes or until cheese softens; stir gently. Season with salt and pepper to taste.

● Divide among lettuce-lined plates. Garnish with radishes and parsley. Makes 4 servings.

Mexican Quesadilla Salad

Half	small red onion, sliced	Half
1	head romaine lettuce	1
3	large tomatoes, diced	3
1	can (19 oz/540 mL) chick-peas, drained and rinsed	1
1-1/3 cups	shredded Cheddar cheese (4 oz/125 g)	325 mL
4	8-inch (20 cm) flour tortillas	4
1/4 cup	chopped fresh coriander (optional)	50 mL
	AVOCADO DRESSING	
3/4 cup	plain yogurt	175 mL
1	large avocado, peeled and pitted	1
1/4 cup	chopped green onions	50 mL
2 tbsp	lime juice	25 mL
1	fresh red chili pepper, chopped	1
1/4 tsp	each salt and pepper	1 mL

● Soak onion in cold water for 15 minutes; drain and pat dry. Separate romaine and tear into bite-size pieces. In bowl, combine onion, romaine, tomatoes, chick-peas and Cheddar.

● AVOCADO DRESSING: In blender or food processor, purée together yogurt, avocado, green onions, lime juice, red chili pepper, salt and pepper until smooth; toss with salad until coated.

● In nonstick skillet, warm tortillas over medium-high heat for 30 seconds on each side or until lightly toasted. Place tortilla on each plate; top with salad. Sprinkle with coriander (if using). Makes 4 servings.

For a big bowlful of Tex-Mex flavor, just toss Cheddar, tomatoes, lettuce and coriander in a guacamole-style dressing and pile onto a tortilla.

RIPENING AN AVOCADO

All avocadoes are shipped rock-hard to avoid bruising and need to be ripened at home. To speed up the process, enclose avocado in a paper bag (with an apple, if you're in a real rush) and let stand at room temperature out of the sun for 2 to 3 days or until the avocado yields to gentle pressure.

Asparagus and Fusilli Toss

1-2/3 cups	fusilli	400 mL
8 oz	asparagus	250 g
2	carrots	2
1 tsp	grated lemon rind	5 mL
3 tbsp	lemon juice	50 mL
2 tbsp	olive oil	25 mL
1 tsp	Dijon mustard	5 mL
1	clove garlic, minced	1
1/4 tsp	salt	1 mL
Pinch	pepper	Pinch
1/3 cup	ricotta cheese	75 mL
1 tbsp	chopped fresh dill	15 mL

● In large pot of boiling salted water, cook fusilli for 8 to 10 minutes or until tender but firm. Drain and refresh under cold water; drain again.

● Meanwhile, trim asparagus and cut into bite-size pieces. Peel and slice carrots into strips. In steamer, cook asparagus and carrots for 4 minutes; refresh under cold water and drain well.

● In large bowl, whisk together lemon rind and juice, oil, mustard, garlic, salt and pepper. Add fusilli, asparagus mixture, ricotta cheese and dill; toss to coat well. Makes 3 servings.

Enjoy the pleasure of spring asparagus in an easy toss of pasta and creamy dill dressing.

Main-Dish Sandwiches

When you're looking for a quick fuss-free meal that will please everyone in the household, it's hard to beat a main-course sandwich. Hot or cold, these stuffed-full-of-flavor buns or slices of bread bring satisfaction any time of day.

Chicken Fajitas ▶

Cumin is a spice that's rising in popularity. The long narrow seeds are usually ground, giving their distinctive flavor to many Mexican, Indian and Middle Eastern dishes. Cumin is also blended into chili powder mixtures.

4	boneless skinless chicken breasts	4
2 tbsp	vegetable oil	25 mL
4	10-inch (25 cm) flour tortillas	4
	Toppings (see box, p. 84)	
	MARINADE	
1 tsp	grated lime rind	5 mL
1/4 cup	lime juice	50 mL
1/4 cup	vegetable oil	50 mL
2 tbsp	Worcestershire sauce	25 mL
1	small onion, minced	1
2	cloves garlic, minced	2
1-1/2 tsp	ground cumin	7 mL
1/2 tsp	salt	2 mL
1/4 tsp	pepper	1 mL
Dash	hot pepper sauce	Dash

● Cut chicken into 1/2-inch (1 cm) wide strips.

● MARINADE: In large bowl, combine lime rind and juice, oil, Worcestershire sauce, onion, garlic, cumin, salt, pepper and hot pepper sauce. Add chicken, stirring to coat. Cover and marinate at room temperature for 30 minutes or in refrigerator for up to 8 hours.

● Drain chicken and pat dry with paper towels. Heat browning dish according to manufacturer's instructions; pour in oil and tilt to coat. Add chicken and stir; microwave at High, stirring twice, for 2 to 2-1/2 minutes or until no longer pink inside. Set aside.

● Wrap tortillas in paper towels; microwave at Medium-High (70%) for 30 seconds or until warm. Place on plates; top with chicken. Drizzle with pan drippings, if desired. Sprinkle with desired toppings; fold over or roll up. Makes 4 servings.

TIP: Instead of microwaving the fajitas, cook the chicken in a skillet in 1 tbsp (15 mL) vegetable oil for about 5 minutes or until no longer pink inside. Wrap the tortillas in foil and warm in 350°F (180°C) oven for 5 minutes.

Hamburger Fajitas

Fajitas are becoming everyone's favorite fast food, and no wonder. Try these tasty ones the next time you need an easy dinner in a hurry.

1 tsp	vegetable oil	5 mL
1	clove garlic, minced	1
1/2 cup	thinly sliced onion	125 mL
8 oz	ground beef	250 g
1/2 cup	thinly sliced sweet red or green pepper	125 mL
1 tsp	Worcestershire sauce	5 mL
1 tsp	lemon juice	5 mL
1/2 tsp	salt	2 mL
1/4 tsp	pepper	1 mL
4	6-inch (15 cm) flour tortillas	4
1/2 cup	tomato salsa	125 mL
	Toppings (see box, below)	

● In skillet, heat oil over medium heat; cook garlic and onion, stirring occasionally, for about 5 minutes or until softened.

● Add beef; cook, breaking up meat with back of spoon, for about 3 minutes or until no longer pink. Add red pepper, Worcestershire sauce, lemon juice, salt and pepper; cook, stirring occasionally, for about 3 minutes or until red pepper is tender-crisp.

● Meanwhile, wrap tortillas in foil; heat in 350°F (180°C) oven for 5 minutes or until warm. Place on plates; top with meat mixture and salsa. Sprinkle with desired toppings; roll up. Makes 2 servings.

Tuna Burritos ▶

A new take on burritos combines tuna, chick-peas and crunchy vegetables in a warm cheesy wrapper. Add a salad and a dab of salsa for supper or lunch in minutes.

1 tbsp	vegetable oil	15 mL
1	onion, chopped	1
2	cloves garlic, minced	2
2	stalks celery, diced	2
1 cup	diced sweet green pepper	250 mL
1	can (19 oz/540 mL) chick-peas	1
2 tsp	chili powder	10 mL
1/2 tsp	each dried oregano and ground cumin	2 mL
1/4 tsp	hot pepper sauce	1 mL
1/4 cup	lemon or lime juice	50 mL
4	10-inch (25 cm) flour tortillas	4
1	can (135 g) tuna, drained	1
1 cup	shredded Cheddar cheese	250 mL

● In large skillet, heat oil over medium heat; cook onion, garlic, celery and 3/4 cup (175 mL) of the green pepper, stirring often, for 5 to 7 minutes or until softened.

● Reserve 1/4 cup (50 mL) of the liquid from chick-peas. Rinse and drain chick-peas; add to skillet along with chili powder, oregano, cumin and hot pepper sauce, mashing with potato masher. Stir in lemon juice and reserved liquid; cook, stirring, until heated through.

● Spread mixture evenly over tortillas, leaving 1-inch (2.5 cm) border; sprinkle with tuna pieces. Roll up and place, seam side down, in greased 13- x 9-inch (3 L) baking dish; cover tightly with foil and bake in 400°F (200°C) oven for 15 minutes.

● Sprinkle with Cheddar; bake, uncovered, for about 3 minutes or until Cheddar has melted. Garnish with remaining green pepper. Makes 4 servings.

TEX-MEX TOPPINGS

Keep a selection of toppings handy, ready to spoon or sprinkle onto fajitas whenever the urge for Tex-Mex strikes.

● sliced red onions and sweet green pepper
● diced avocado or guacamole

● chopped tomatoes
● shredded Iceberg lettuce

● shredded Cheddar cheese
● sour cream
● chopped fresh coriander

● taco sauce
● black olives
● salsa

LINGO LESSON

If you're confused by all the Tex-Mex terminology, here's the key to what you're cooking.

● **Tortillas:** Flat, round wheat-flour bread found in the frozen or refrigerated foods section of the supermarket.

● **Burritos:** Tortillas filled and rolled into a cigar shape, then usually baked.

● **Quesadillas:** Tortillas filled and folded like a turnover, then grilled or griddle-cooked. Cheese is often included as a main ingredient.

● **Fajitas:** Tortillas folded around a spicy fried mix of meat and vegetables.

Sloppy Sausage Joes

Make-ahead recipes are perfect for on-the-go households where a ready-to-thaw dish is like an ace in the hole on busy evenings. This family favorite is also great for packing frozen into a cooler, to thaw slowly as you drive away camping or cottaging.

12 oz	sweet Italian sausage	375 g
2 tsp	vegetable oil	10 mL
12 oz	lean ground beef	375 g
2	onions, chopped	2
1	sweet pepper, chopped	1
1	zucchini, chopped	1
1 cup	sliced mushrooms (4 oz/125 g)	250 mL
3	cloves garlic, minced	3
1 tsp	dried oregano	5 mL
3	tomatoes, chopped	3
2 tbsp	tomato paste	25 mL
1/2 tsp	salt	2 mL
1/4 tsp	pepper	1 mL
6	kaiser rolls	6

● Remove casings from sausage. In Dutch oven, heat oil over medium-high heat; cook beef and sausage, breaking up meat with back of spoon, for about 5 minutes or until no longer pink. Using slotted spoon, remove and set aside.

● Drain off fat from pan. Cook onions and sweet pepper, stirring occasionally, for 2 minutes. Add zucchini, mushrooms, garlic and oregano; cook for 4 minutes.

● Return meat to pan along with tomatoes, tomato paste, salt and pepper; bring to boil. Reduce heat and simmer, stirring occasionally, for about 20 minutes or until vegetables are tender. *(Sauce can be cooled in refrigerator and frozen in airtight container for up to 1 month; thaw and reheat gently to serve.)*

● Slice rolls in half horizontally almost through; spoon sauce into rolls. Makes 6 servings.

Salad-Bar Subs

A sub can't be a sub if it isn't generously mounded with messy but delicious fillings. Gather the gang and dig in — just make sure you have plenty of serviettes on hand!

8	slices bacon	8
4	hard-cooked eggs	4
1/4 cup	light mayonnaise	50 mL
2	green onions, sliced	2
	Salt and pepper	
4	submarine rolls	4
2 tbsp	Dijon mustard	25 mL
8	lettuce leaves	8
2	tomatoes, thinly sliced	2
Half	cucumber, thinly sliced	Half
1/2 cup	alfalfa sprouts	125 mL

● In skillet, cook bacon over high heat until crisp; drain on paper towels.

● In bowl, chop eggs; mix in mayonnaise, onions, and salt and pepper to taste.

● Slice rolls in half lengthwise almost through. Spread cut sides with mustard; tuck lettuce leaf into each roll. Evenly spoon in egg mixture; top with tomato, cucumber, sprouts and bacon. Makes 4 servings.

TIP: To hard-cook eggs, place eggs in saucepan that holds them comfortably and cover with cold water to 1 inch (2.5 cm) above the shells. Bring to boil over medium-high heat. Immediately cover, remove from heat and let stand for 18 minutes. Drain and chill in copious amounts of cold water. For easy removal of shell, crack and shell eggs under water.

Confetti Pepper Muffuletta ▼

1	each sweet red, green and yellow pepper, finely diced	1
1/4 cup	chopped Kalamata or oil-cured black olives	50 mL
3 tbsp	chopped fresh parsley	45 mL
2 tbsp	drained capers	25 mL
3	anchovy fillets, minced (or 4 tsp/20 mL anchovy paste)	3
3	cloves garlic, minced	3
1 tsp	dried oregano	5 mL
2/3 cup	extra virgin olive oil	150 mL
1	round (8-inch/20 cm) Italian or French loaf	1
4 oz	thinly sliced salami	125 g
4 oz	thinly sliced provolone or mozzarella cheese	125 g
4 oz	thinly sliced mortadella or ham	125 g

TIP: Our recipe is geared to an 8-inch (20 cm) crusty loaf, but loaves a bit larger are just as good, although the filling will not be as high. You can also use a long crusty loaf, cutting it into wide slices to serve.

● In bowl, combine peppers, olives, parsley, capers, anchovies, garlic and oregano; pour in oil and toss to combine. Cover and refrigerate overnight. Drain, reserving liquid.

● Slice bread in half horizontally; hollow out insides, leaving 1-inch (2.5 cm) thick walls. Brush inside of bread with reserved liquid.

● Spoon half of the pepper mixture into bottom shell. Layer with salami, provolone and mortadella, packing to edge of bread cavity. Top with remaining pepper mixture, mounding in center. Replace top half of bread; wrap well. Weigh down with can in refrigerator for 30 minutes or for up to 8 hours. Unwrap and cut into wedges. Makes 8 servings.

Muffuletta is a New Orleans meal of cold meats, cheese and olive salad in a bun that's so big it's actually a round loaf of bread. The whole-stuffed loaf is make-ahead and ideal for parties or picnics as well as suppers and lunches.

Vegetarian No-Fry Falafels

Falafels, Middle Eastern chick-pea patties, are usually deep-fried. But here, they're baked, then popped into pitas with a yogurt-vegetable salad and simply enjoyed. A word of warning, though — this meal-in-a-pouch is very juicy and needs to be eaten over a large plate with many serviettes!

1/3 cup	bulgur	75 mL
2	cloves garlic, halved	2
1	can (19 oz/540 mL) chick-peas, drained and rinsed	1
1	small onion, coarsely chopped	1
1 cup	cubed whole wheat bread	250 mL
2 tbsp	lemon juice	25 mL
1 tsp	ground cumin	5 mL
1/2 tsp	ground coriander	2 mL
1/4 tsp	each salt and pepper	1 mL
Dash	hot pepper sauce	Dash
1/2 cup	chopped fresh parsley	125 mL
2 tbsp	vegetable oil	25 mL
2	whole wheat pita breads	2
	TOPPING	
1/2 cup	plain yogurt	125 mL
1 tsp	lemon juice	5 mL
2	small cloves garlic, minced	2
2	tomatoes, chopped	2
1	small onion, sliced	1
4	lettuce leaves	4

● In bowl, pour about 2 cups (500 mL) boiling water over bulgur; let stand for 30 minutes. Drain; squeeze out excess moisture.

● In food processor, mince garlic. Add bulgur, chick-peas, onion, bread, lemon juice, cumin, coriander, salt, pepper and hot pepper sauce; purée for 1 minute or until smooth. Stir in parsley.

● Scoop out twelve 1/4-cup (50 mL) mounds onto well-greased baking sheet; flatten into patties about 1/2 inch (1 cm) thick. (Mixture will be sticky.) Bake in 400°F (200°C) oven for 10 minutes on each side or until firm.

● Brush patties with oil; broil for about 2 minutes per side or until golden and crisp. *(Patties can be cooled in refrigerator and stored in airtight container for up to 2 days; reheat, covered, in 400°F/200°C oven for 10 minutes or until hot.)*

● TOPPING: Combine yogurt, lemon juice and garlic. Cut each pita in half; open to form pouch. Nestle each patty into pouch along with tomatoes, onion and lettuce. Drizzle with sauce. Makes 4 servings.

Grilled Cheese French Toast

On a too-tired-to-cook night, just keep the fixings for this soul-warming sandwich on hand, and supper's well on its way. Serve with chunky salsa or sliced tomatoes.

4	slices bread	4
1 tbsp	Dijon mustard	15 mL
4 oz	Cheddar or Swiss cheese, sliced	125 g
2	thin slices ham	2
2	eggs	2
1/4 cup	milk	50 mL
Pinch	each salt and pepper	Pinch
2 tsp	butter	10 mL
1 tsp	vegetable oil	5 mL

● Spread one side of each bread slice with mustard. Evenly arrange Cheddar and ham over 2 of the slices; sandwich with remaining bread.

● In shallow dish, whisk together eggs, milk, salt and pepper. Add sandwiches, one at a time, turning to soak up mixture.

● In skillet, melt butter with oil over medium heat; cook sandwiches for about 3 minutes on each side or until golden brown and cheese has melted. Makes 2 servings.

Crunchy Fish Burgers ▲

2 tbsp	all-purpose flour	25 mL
1/2 tsp	each dried basil and salt	2 mL
1/4 tsp	pepper	1 mL
1	egg	1
1 tbsp	vegetable oil	15 mL
2 cups	flaked corn cereal, crushed	500 mL
1 lb	fish fillets	500 g
4	whole wheat rolls	4
3 tbsp	light mayonnaise	50 mL
2 tbsp	pickle relish	25 mL
1/2 tsp	lemon juice	2 mL
Pinch	cayenne pepper	Pinch
4	lettuce leaves	4
2	tomatoes, sliced	2

● In shallow dish, mix together flour, basil, salt and pepper. In separate dish, beat egg with oil. Place cereal in third shallow dish.

● Cut fish into pieces to fit rolls. Dip each piece into flour mixture. Dip into egg mixture, then into cereal, pressing to coat both sides.

● Bake on greased baking sheet in 450°F (230°C) oven, turning once, for 6 to 8 minutes or until golden and fish flakes easily when tested with fork.

● Meanwhile, slice rolls in half horizontally; open and toast in oven for about 4 minutes or until crisp. Combine mayonnaise, relish, lemon juice and cayenne. Layer bottom half of each roll with lettuce, fish, mayonnaise mixture and tomatoes. Top with remaining roll. Makes 4 servings.

If you love the crunch of deep-fried fish but hate all that fat and smelly deep-frying, these oven-baked fish fillets nestled in buns with special sauce and lots of tomatoes and lettuce are your dream come true.

The Contributors

For your easy reference, we have included an alphabetical listing of recipes by contributor.

Claire Arfin
New Orleans Hands-On
    Supper, 58

Carla Azevedo
Big-Batch Portuguese
    Pumpkin Soup, 70

Elizabeth Baird
A Real Bargain of a Cabbage
    Soup, 62
Bean Bag Vegetable
    Soup, 65
BLT Salad, 74
Braised Lamb Shanks with
    Beans, 56
Cape Breton Fish
    Chowder, 69
Cheese and Mushroom
    Perogy Casserole, 19
Chowder-Style Mussels, 58
Crunchy Fish Burgers, 89
Crusty Chicken
    Cassoulet, 17
Curried Squash Stew, 60
Potato Broccoli Chowder, 68
Red Bean and Lamb
    Salad, 74

Fran Berkoff
Asparagus and Fusilli
    Toss, 81

Johanna Burkhard
Spicy Lamb Stew, 56
Vegetable Cobbler, 30

Vicki Burns
Cheesy Tuna Doubles, 28
Creole Sausage and
    Peppers, 11
Pork Chili with Squash and
    Beans, 55
Vegetarian Moussaka
    Doubles, 22
Vegetarian No-Fry
    Falafels, 88

Pam Collacott
Hamburger Fajitas, 84

Cynthia David
Red Pepper Cheese
    Quiche, 26

Nancy Enright
Paella, 40

Margaret Fraser
Autumn Harvest Soup, 70
Burgundy Beef, 50
Chicken and Scallop Pad
    Thai, 43
Parsleyed Rice Ring, 51
Rösti with Cheese and
    Spinach, 45
Stir-Fried Turkey and
    Fiddleheads, 37

Barb Holland
Hoisin Fish and Vegetable
    Medley, 40

Heather Howe
Hamburger Goulash
    Soup, 71
Lentil Barley Potage, 71

Marion Kane
Spicy Rice and Beans, 27
Tofu Ratatouille, 25

Anne Lindsay
Chick-Pea and Tomato Stew
    with Basil, 61

Lisbeth Lodge
Herbed Vegetables with Eggs
    and Toast, 44

Helen Bishop MacDonald
Marsetti, 19

Rose Murray
Apple Sauerkraut Pork
    Chops, 39
Chicken Pie with Phyllo
    Crust, 32
Chicken Shepherd's Pie, 36
Daube of Beef with
    Orange, 51
Eggs Creole, 29
Fiesta Mac and Cheese, 21
Grilled Cheese French
    Toast, 88
Orange Teriyaki Roast
    Pork, 54
Quick Chunky
    Minestrone, 65
Salad-Bar Subs, 86
Stuffed Squash with Ham
    and Rice, 10
Tex-Mex Potato
    Casserole, 14
Tuna Burritos, 84

Ruth Phelan
Grilled Chicken Salad, 77

Daphna Rabinovitch
Corn and Cheddar
  Chowder, 68

Michelle Ramsay
Caribbean Chicken Salad, 78
Mediterranean Couscous
  Salad, 75
Mexican Quesadilla
  Salad, 81
Warm Beef Stir-Fry
  Salad, 72

Iris Raven
Make-Ahead Penne
  Salad, 79
Mini Beef Pot Pies, 33
Pork with Snow Peas and
  Couscous for One, 38
Quick Skillet Beef Stew for
  One, 37
Souffléed Ham, Swiss
  Cheese and Squash, 10

Edena Sheldon
Chicken and Pear Salad, 76

Bonnie Stern
Polenta with Beef and
  Sausage Ragout, 52
Roast Lamb with
  Potatoes, 54
Shepherd's Pie with Garlic
  Mashed Potatoes, 15
Spaghetti Tuna Salad, 75
Tofu Vegetable Stir-Fry, 45

Anita Stewart
Smoky Bean Soup, 64

Bev Witton
Vegetarian Chili, 61

Canadian Living Test Kitchen
All-New Oven Stew, 48
Asparagus Lasagna, 18
Big-Batch Impossible
  Broccoli Pie, 26
Chicken Fajitas, 82
Confetti Pepper
  Muffuletta, 87
Corn, Bean and Beef
  Casserole, 8
Country Cabbage Rolls, 6
Couscous and Chick-Pea
  Salad, 79
Crunchy Crouton
  Quiche, 24

Curried Beef Stew, 48
Easy Chicken Stir-Fry, 34
Fast-Lane Chicken Pot
  Pie, 30
Lentil Pepper Ragout on
  Herbed Couscous, 60
Meatballs in Sweet and Sour
  Sauce, 52
Mediterranean Fish Soup
  with Croutes, 67
Microwave Chinese Chicken
  and Rice, 16
Orange Beef Stir-Fry, 34
Party-Size Baked Vegetable
  Spaghetti, 20
Pasta Shrimp Salad for a
  Crowd, 78
Perfect Pastry Every
  Time, 33
Pizza Popover, 14
Quick Curried Lamb, 39
Shepherd's Hash Brown
  Pie, 9
Shrimp Vegetable
  Stir-Fry, 42
Sloppy Sausage Joes, 86
Speedy Choucroute
  Garni, 12
Tomato Clam Chowder, 66
Two-Cheese and Corn
  Baked Risotto, 25
Warm Potato Salad with
  Brie, 80

Photography Credits

FRED BIRD: front and back
covers, introduction, 7, 13,
18, 19, 21, 23, 24, 27, 29, 32,
35, 36, 38, 41, 43, 44, 49, 50,
53, 57, 63, 64, 66, 69, 73, 77,
80, 85, 87, 89.

CHRISTOPHER
CAMPBELL: 16, 59, 75.

LINDA CORBETT: 9, 31.

CURTIS TRENT: front flap.

MIKE VISSER: 83.

Special Thanks

Acknowledging the people who have made *Canadian Living's Best One-Dish Meals* is a pleasure. The creativity, patience and organizing skills of Madison Press project editor Wanda Nowakowska are first in line for appreciation, as are Beverley Renahan, meticulous *Canadian Living* senior editor, and Daphna Rabinovitch, talented manager of *Canadian Living's* Test Kitchen. Others at the magazine are due sincere thanks as well: Test Kitchen staff shown on the front flap, plus Donna Bartolini, Jennifer MacKenzie and Dana McCauley, as well as senior editor Donna Paris. Our "looks good enough to eat" photography comes largely via the skills of art director Deborah Fadden, food stylists Olga Truchan and Jennifer McLagan and photographer Fred Bird, and the clean user-friendly design from Gord Sibley. Wonderful home cooking across Canada is all the easier and more delicious because of the contributions of *Canadian Living's* very accomplished and valued food writers, noted across the page. Of course, all of our work at *Canadian Living* is under the guidance of editor-in-chief Bonnie Cowan and publisher Kirk Shearer, whose commitment to *The Best* series is wonderful encouragement.

Elizabeth Baird

Index

Over 100 simple, satisfying and convenient recipes.

Look to *Canadian Living* for all of THE BEST!

More than 100 quick pasta sauces and tosses, hearty soups, salads and baked entrées, Oriental noodle dishes and vegetarian pasta are featured here in easy-to-follow recipes.

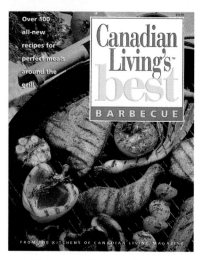

Add some exciting new flavors to your outdoor cooking with the tastiest marinades for meat and fish plus tempting appetizers, vegetables — even pizzas and quesadillas!

More than 100 new ways to cook this family favorite — from skillet suppers and stir-fries to one-pot chicken dinners, soups, salads and dressed-up dishes for company.

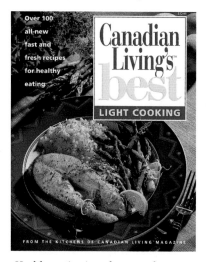

Healthy eating is a pleasure when you can enjoy such delicious recipes as *Celery and Sage Pork Roast* and *Buttermilk Mashed Potatoes* with *Strawberry Citrus Charlotte* for dessert.

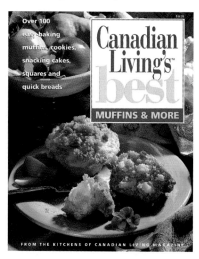

From sweet to savory to make-ahead mixes — all these muffins take just minutes to prepare. You'll also find easy-to-bake cupcakes, biscuits, cookies and cakes.

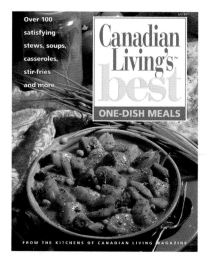

Wonderful recipes for satisfying casseroles and stews— along with quick and easy stir-fries, main-course salads and soups, plus super-sized sandwiches and ever popular pasta.

WATCH FOR MORE NEW BOOKS IN THE MONTHS AHEAD... FROM *CANADIAN LIVING* SO YOU KNOW THEY'RE —THE BEST!